"Hey, babe, wanna roll out to Stillwell Beach and drink a few beers?"

Stephanie spun around and looked up into the deep-set, black eyes of Kirk Wa... I'm going to the swim meet," ...

"Since ... ned about our dear ... n tightly. "What's ... ot good enough fo...

"Get you...

"Hey, tha... jailbird . . ."

Stephanie ... she said, her voice small and pleading, please don't start blabbing about my past around school. It would ruin everything."

"I bet it would," he said, turning to her. "So what do I get if I keep my mouth shut?"

Stephanie looked at him helplessly. "I don't know. I don't have much to offer."

"You got plenty in my book," he said with a chuckle that sent spasms of fear down her back. "Now get in the car."

Meet Glenwood High's fabulous four, the

SENIORS

Kit, Elaine, Alex, and Lori are very best friends.
Every girl's ideal, every boy's dream. These popular seniors share all their hopes, fears, and deepest secrets.

On the brink of graduation and adulthood, they're discovering themselves, planning for the future . . . and falling in love. Don't miss them!

Ask your bookseller for titles you have missed:

1. TOO MUCH, TOO SOON
2. SMART ENOUGH TO KNOW
3. WINNER ALL THE WAY
4. AFRAID TO LOVE
5. BEFORE IT'S TOO LATE
6. TOO HOT TO HANDLE
7. HANDS OFF HE'S MINE
8. FORBIDDEN KISSES
9. A TOUCH OF GINGER
10. PRESENTING SUPERHUNK

Coming soon:

12. DON'T SAY GOODBYE

SENIORS™

BAD GIRL

by Eileen Goudge

BANTAM BOOKS

TORONTO • NEW YORK • LONDON • SYDNEY • AUCKLAND

BAD GIRL

A Bantam Book / July 1987

Cover photo by Pat Hill.

ISBN 0-553-17373-1

Bantam Books are published by Bantam Books, Inc. Its trademark, consisting of the words "Bantam Books" and the portrayal of a rooster, is Registered in U.S. Patent and Trademark Office and in other countries. Marca Registrada. Bantam Books, Inc., 666 Fifth Avenue, New York, New York 10103.

Printed and bound in Great Britain by
Cox & Wyman Ltd., Reading

O 0 9 8 7 6 5 4 3 2 1

Chapter One

"Alex, you mustn't tell anyone," begged Stephanie, her large coppery eyes wide with fear. She let her long brown hair hide her face, as she picked nervously at the counterpane. "... Please."

"But the whole gang already knows," Alex protested. "They were as excited about your arrival as I was."

"Then we've just got to swear them to secrecy," countered Stephanie.

"How?" Alex said, frustration edging into her voice. "Not that they won't agree to keep it a secret, but what are they ... we ... supposed to tell everyone else when they ask? I can't just say you dropped in from Mars one evening. And everyone knows I don't really have a sister."

"You're the one who likes challenges," snapped Stephanie. "You come up with something. I just don't want people to know the truth. Not yet. I'm not ready."

"Okay, but you don't have to yell at me," Alex threw out.

"I'm not yelling!" Stephanie shouted back before she could stop herself. Quickly, she turned away from Alex, toward the window, twisting her fingers nervously. She could feel tears threatening to break free. She didn't mean to snap at Alex but she was scared. Shouting, she knew, would disguise the tremor in her voice.

Stephanie continued to stare out the window, her shoulders rigid, her posture defiant. More than anything she didn't want her past, her background, coming out. Before it hadn't mattered. Before she'd almost flaunted it—the foster homes, her success in running away, the night in jail. But she'd never had Rick Forrester before. Rick Forrester, the boy from probably the best family in Glenwood—certainly from one of the richest. The Forresters' family history was the very fabric from which Glenwood was made. And actually she didn't really "have" him. But he seemed interested in her, and she didn't want to blow it. Not this time.

"Ah, Steph," said Alex, patting her foster sister awkwardly on the shoulder. "I wish you weren't so uptight about the past. That's behind you. You've got a whole new life in Glenwood. Don't worry about what people will think. Let them judge you by the way you act now, okay?"

Stephanie sighed deeply. Good old Alex. She was

trying to make things better. As usual. But Alex didn't realize what was at stake, and Stephanie didn't feel like telling her. Her feelings for Rick were so new and confusing, she hadn't even figured it all out herself. So the last thing she wanted was for someone to step in and try to make things smooth for her. Despite Alex's good intentions, it would just screw everything up. No, Rick Forrester she wanted to handle in her own way, in her own time.

"Look," said Stephanie finally, her voice thin and distant. "Why can't we just tell people I'm your cousin who's staying with you for a while?"

"Yeah . . . ?" Alex replied expectantly.

"Well, it worked for Ginger, didn't it?" asked Stephanie defensively. "She told everyone she was staying with her cousin Kit while her mother went to some cooking school in Paris."

"Right. The only difference is, Ginger's story is true," Alex replied evenly.

Stephanie flinched. *Lies again.* Would her life always be a series of deceptions? The lies she told to get out of trouble invariably seemed to lead her back into trouble. She paused, weighing the alternatives. Then she shrugged. No, this time she couldn't take a chance on the truth—it could only hurt her.

"Okay, so let's say I'm staying with you while my mother tours Europe," Stephanie said decisively.

"Doing what? Teaching gourmet cooking to people like Ginger's mother?" asked Alex rolling her eyes.

"No. She's an opera singer. Say she's an opera singer. Don't they have to go off on tours all the time?"

"Yes..." hesitated Alex, then she turned and stared directly at Stephanie. "Okay, Steph. If this is the way you want it, I'll go along with you. I'll talk to the gang this afternoon. I just hope that one day you get comfortable with your life, with who you are, even who you're not...or else you're never going to be happy."

Stephanie scarcely heard the last of what Alex said, she was so relieved that her foster sister had agreed not to squeal on her. Her past was safely locked away. At least for a while. That's all she cared about right now.

"Thanks, Alex. Thanks a lot," she said, her breath coming out in a rush of relief.

"Sure. What's a sister for anyway?" Alex replied lightly, jumping off the bed. "And if I don't get in the shower right now, we'll never get to school." She bounced out the door, leaving Stephanie sitting on her bed staring out the window.

It was the squeak of the shower being turned off that finally brought Stephanie out of her black thoughts of the past to the present comfort of the Enomotos' home. She looked around with a shock, as if realizing for the first time how lucky she was to have been found by the Enomotos. She had a beautiful home and a room all to herself and...she glared at the clock—school to go to!!! It was eight o'clock; she and Alex had to leave in thirty minutes, and she didn't want to be late. Today everything had to go just perfectly.

"Uh...Alex," called Stephanie down the hall. "Can I...May I borrow that blouse you wore last week?" She hesitated, then added with a rush, "You know, the one you had on at the racetrack?"

"Sure," Alex shouted back. "Come on down."

Again Stephanie hesitated. Would she ever get used to asking for things? It just didn't come naturally. She picked through the meager collection in her closet once more, pulling out a few old blouses and holding them up in front of the mirror, but nothing was right. Today she wanted to look extra nice. Today she needed Alex's shirt, the one with the wide blue-and-white stripes. It was exactly right.

She hurried down the hall. Alex was still in the bathroom, so Stephanie sat down to wait, letting her eyes take in the sunny yellow room around her. The walls were plastered with posters and the bookshelves crammed with trophies and medals, all thrown haphazardly together. She couldn't help noticing how boring her own room was in comparison. It still looked as it did the day she moved in three months ago—neat, but featureless, lacking any personal touches, unless Noodle's chess trophy could be considered a personal touch. She still wasn't sure what had made her drag it out of the closet and put it up. Was it knowing it had belonged to Alex's brother, someone she had loved so much? Was it knowing he was dead? Sometimes it scared her to see how sentimental she could be.

"Here it is," said Alex, coming through the door and going to the closet to pull out the blouse. Her straight black hair was still damp from the shower, and the dark, almond-shaped eyes that bespoke her Japanese heritage sparkled with an intensity that was typically Alex. Stephanie admired the athletic grace with which her "sister" moved around the cluttered room.

Boy, if I had a single drop of her talent, or just one of those diving medals up there, I'd be so proud I'd bust, thought Stephanie. Maybe I'll pretend Noodle's trophy is really mine, one I've earned for being good at something. *Ha! Fat chance, kid*, she scolded herself. *You got to have talent to win trophies, and we all know your talents add up to a clean zero.*

"Uh . . . maybe I have something in my own closet after all," stammered Stephanie, getting up and moving toward the door.

Alex eyed her sharply. "Stephanie, I want you to have that blouse . . . please."

The two girls stared at each other for a moment. Suddenly Alex broke into a wide grin. "But only if you promise not to look absolutely gorgeous in it."

Stephanie smiled back. The tension was gone. "I don't think you have to worry about that. Thanks." She took the blouse and disappeared back down the hall. Slowly she buttoned it up, savoring the feel of the expensive cloth against her skin, and tucked it into her slim-fitting jeans.

"Wow! That looks great," Alex called from the doorway, on her way to breakfast.

Stephanie grinned shyly. "You don't think it makes me look fat the way it bags around the waist?"

"Chic, yes—fat, no way," Alex said. "What's the big occasion?"

Stephanie turned away defensively and began pulling a brush roughly through her straight brown hair. She noticed that the decent diet she'd had since moving in with the Enomotos had turned her hair from lank and dull to thick and shiny. It was almost pretty.

"Doesn't have anything to do with the sock hop at lunch today, does it?" Alex prodded. "And that gorgeous hunk Rick Forrester?"

Stephanie wished Alex would just go away. Her relationship with Rick was too new, her feelings too raw to talk about it. She pulled the brush through her hair one more time, then dabbed on some mascara.

"I don't know why you wear that stuff," Alex commented. "Your eyelashes are already as thick as paintbrushes."

"Maybe I just want to," snapped Stephanie, immediately regretting her outburst.

"Uh-oh, I think I get the message: Enomoto... clam up! Right?"

"Oh, Alex, I'm sorry," said Stephanie. "I didn't mean to bite your head off. I guess I'm just kind of uptight about today. I mean I've hardly seen Rick since the senior costume party. Everything was so perfect then. Maybe he won't even show at the dance today." She hesitated, biting nervously at her full lower lip. "He asked me if I was going. Don't you think that means he's interested in meeting me there?"

"Sounds like it to me," Alex agreed. "Just relax. I bet he'll be there. He sure seemed to like you a lot at that costume party."

Stephanie blushed. "Uh... what time's your swim meet today?"

"Three-thirty. Why?"

"I don't know. I just thought if I had nothing to do,

I'd stop by and see what the diving demon of Glenwood High looks like in action."

"Oh, Steph! Really?" bubbled Alex. "You mean you'll really come to the meet?"

"Hey, I said I might," added Stephanie quickly. "I don't want to commit myself."

"Sure . . . I understand," Alex said equally as fast.

The girls went down to breakfast in silence. Stephanie couldn't deny that the Enomotos were the best foster family she'd ever had, and after six tries, that was saying something. It still felt weird sometimes, though, not to be free, not to be able to stick out her thumb and split whenever she wanted. Maybe she'd take off for a weekend; just by herself. See if the open road still had that old magic.

"Good morning, girls," Dr. Enomoto called cheerfully over the top of his newspaper when Alex and Stephanie entered the kitchen. The smell of cooking bacon hung thickly in the air making Stephanie's stomach growl with hunger.

"Hi ya, Dad," returned Alex, sitting down beside him and pouring herself a big bowl of granola. "Hi, Mom."

"Hello, dear. Hello, Stephanie," Mrs. Enomoto sang out from the stove.

"You girls are cutting your time pretty close this morning, aren't you?" asked Dr. Enomoto, his dark eyes twinkling with good humor.

Stephanie just smiled as she took her seat. She liked Dr. Enomoto. He was taller than most Japanese men and quite good looking, too. But his eyes were what really got to her. They were so kind and trusting—like Rick's. A shiver ran down Stephanie's back. When Rick smiled, his eyes went all crinkly and warm. During those moments, Stephanie almost felt safe.

"So, Dad, anything happening in the world that we should know about before venturing out?" teased Alex, ignoring his question.

"As a matter of fact, yes," he said seriously, giving the paper a determined snap. "Seems that chlorine has been found to cause cancer. Big article all about it on page two. Says the Food and Drug Administration has closed all swimming pools until further notice."

"What!" gasped Alex in horror.

But Stephanie saw the glint of humor in Dr. Enomoto's eye and started to giggle. He winked at her.

Alex looked from one to the other, then smiled sheepishly. They all burst out laughing with Mrs. Enomoto joining in.

"Someone finally give you a bit of your own medicine, Alex?" quipped Mrs. Enomoto. "How's it feel?"

"Terrible," groaned Alex in mock distress. "But you've got to admit, Dad was really going for the jugular with that one. No fair."

Dr. Enomoto reached over and rumpled Alex's hair. Alex playfully swatted at his hand. A stab of pain went through Stephanie as she watched. If only she had a real father to joke around with. At that moment an old thought reappeared and began to nag again at her. Maybe she really should try to find her parents. At least her mother. She had no recollection of her father, but she had a vague memory of sitting on her mother's lap, listening to her sing children's songs. She could only have been three or four, but she still remembered her mother's beautiful clear voice. Maybe her mother really was an opera singer. Maybe she was out there somewhere looking for Stephanie. Maybe . . .

Suddenly Dr. Enomoto turned and slapped her lightly on the shoulder.

"I might have fooled Alex for a second," he said, "but I didn't get anything by old Steph here. She picked right up on my joke."

Stephanie felt the blood rush to her cheeks but she smiled gratefully at Dr. Enomoto. He was always trying to make her feel good. They all were. Maybe one day she'd be able to relax and just accept it. But right now she was still a little gun-shy of foster families. The last one had come right out and told her they'd only taken her in for the money. Stephanie shuddered at the thought as, despite herself, unpleasant memories of other foster homes crowded into her mind. And the stupid police never had understood why she kept running away!

"You look very nice today, Stephanie," said Mrs. Enomoto, pouring another round of orange juice for everyone.

"Thanks," murmured Stephanie, concentrating on her bowl of cornflakes and hiding her burning cheeks behind a wall of hair.

"It's Alex's blouse," she added.

"Well, just let me know when you want to go shopping, and I'll take you down to the mall where you can pick out some new blouses—or whatever you want—of your own," Mrs. Enomoto offered, probably for the tenth time since Stephanie had come to live with them.

Stephanie nodded, but she had no intention of taking up Mrs. Enomoto on her offer. She simply wasn't ready for more charity. Living in their house, eating their food was about all she could handle right now. She didn't want to be more of a burden.

"You girls have a nice day," continued Mrs. Enomoto brightly. "And Daddy and I'll see you at the meet. Are you going, Stephanie?"

"I'm thinking about it," Stephanie said, throwing on her tattered army jacket.

"Well, we'll look out for you and save a seat."

Mrs. Enomoto gave them both a kiss and bustled them out the front door.

"Ah, rats!" said Alex, standing in the driveway and searching through her baggy fatigue pants. "Where'd I put my keys?"

"Weren't they by the door where you usually throw them?" asked Stephanie.

"I didn't see them when we passed, but maybe I'm still asleep."

"I'll go look."

"Great. I'd check my rucksack but that could take me the rest of the day."

Stephanie giggled and ran back to the house. The keys weren't by the door, or in Alex's room.

"No luck," she said, returning to Alex and her old bomb, the Green Demon.

"How do you feel about walking to school this morning?" asked Alex ruefully.

Stephanie concentrated on the ground. "Want me to hot wire it?"

Alex stared at her openmouthed.

"Well, you've got to admit, driving would sure beat

walking," Stephanie added a little defensively.

"You mean . . . you mean, you really know how?" Alex burst out finally.

"Sure, you'd be surprised what you learn in . . ." Stephanie stopped before adding, "jail." Alex knew. She'd told her once—had bragged about it, but it didn't seem so cool anymore. What would Rick say? Stephanie shuddered. Rick must never find out about her background. Never.

"That's neat," continued Alex, unaware of Stephanie's private thoughts. "Will you teach me?"

"Sure, nothing to it," replied Stephanie. Opening the door, she reached under the dashboard and pulled two wires into view. "Hand me your wire clippers and we'll be under way in two secs."

Dumbfounded but obedient, Alex handed her the greasy clippers from the battered toolbox on the back seat. Stephanie snipped the wires in two, then held the raw edges together. The engine coughed once, then twice, and finally sprang to life.

"Stephanie, you're a genius!" cried Alex, pounding her foster sister on the back. "That's so neat! Wait'll I show Wes. I'll knock his socks off."

Stephanie laughed.

"Let's go," sang out Alex. The two girls jumped in the car and roared off.

The dance was going full blast when Stephanie sidled up to the gym door. She'd never been to one of Glenwood High's noontime events and just hoped everyone had forgotten how dumb she'd said they were. She paid her dollar to the guy collecting at the door. The big poster behind him said, "Dance today so someone can waltz off to college tomorrow." *Clever*, thought Stephanie, stepping warily inside. *At least I'm supporting a good cause*. This was the second dance the Pep Squad had put on this semester to raise money for their special scholarship fund. It was given to a deserving senior on awards night. Someone who was planning to study communications.

Stephanie peered around the gym shyly. The place was packed. Why hadn't Rick asked to meet her someplace else? Maybe he didn't want to make it seem like they were really together. After all, they'd never gone out on a real date. They'd just kind of ended up in the same place and had a good time. Maybe that was all he wanted.

"Stephanie! Hi! Over here!"

Stephanie immediately recognized Lori's slender, graceful arm waving above the crowd. With a sigh of relief, she worked her way over. Lori and Elaine were standing together, watching the people dance.

"Hi, Steph," said Elaine. "What brings you into the jungle on such a nice day?"

Stephanie smiled. Elaine's straightforward, no-nonsense approach to things always put her at ease.

"Uh . . . just thought I'd check out the action," she said. "Looks like a pretty wild time."

"Yeah, just look at Kit," Elaine continued, pointing to a group of boys. Kit was in the middle, dancing up a storm, her soft blond curls a golden blur around her head, her big blue eyes smiling teasingly up at her admirers.

"No wonder she got a dance scholarship to Julliard," said Lori, flicking her long, straight blond hair back over her shoulder. Her eyes were widely set and expressive. If Lori's gentle nature could stand the tough world of modeling, Stephanie figured she'd have no trouble becoming the top-notch model she dreamed of being one day. Her every movement had an unconscious elegance, and she seemed really happy and relaxed these days. Alex had told Stephanie about the older, divorced man Lori had gotten involved with after her boyfriend, Perry, moved to Boston. That must have been a pretty heavy trip dating a man with a little kid, Stephanie thought. Lori was too young and vulnerable for that. Good thing she'd finally realized it, too.

"She really is good," Stephanie agreed, watching Kit's well-developed but highly toned body leap and whirl in rhythm to the fast music.

"Look! Here come Ginger and Fred," observed Elaine, and they all giggled. Gayle Rogers and Bruce Fletcher glided by doing some 1930s number. They'd been dating ever since their successful Ginger Rogers and Fred Astaire routine took the Senior Follies by storm.

Stephanie remembered the night well, since it had been the first time Rick Forrester had shown any real romantic interest in her. Oh, he'd given her a couple of rides in his sexy, cherry red Ferrari before, but that night had been special. He'd made her feel important, like he really cared. Well, if he cared so much, where was he now?

"Where's Carl?" she asked Elaine, to divert herself from thoughts that Rick had stood her up.

"Who knows?" replied Elaine, rolling her eyes in mock exasperation. "He probably programmed himself into his computer and can't figure out how to get back out. I certainly don't see him here."

At five foot nine Elaine had a good vantage point from which to survey the crowd. Stephanie was tempted to ask her if she could look for Rick but decided against it in the end. She didn't want anyone to know how she felt about her handsome classmate until Rick made his feelings clear. She wasn't going to be made a fool of . . . ever again.

"Uh-oh," said Elaine. "Here comes Glenwood's answer to perpetual motion."

Alex bounded up, her eyes sparkling. Behind her walked Rick. Stephanie felt her heart race. He looked wonderful in his faded jeans, old moccasins, and tailored white shirt that contrasted beautifully with his tanned features and mop of soft brown curls. His eyes were the color of melted chocolate.

"Look who I found wandering around," said Alex casually.

Oh, no, thought Stephanie, her stomach dropping suddenly. Alex had dragged him over. Another one of her good-will acts. She shot Alex an angry glance. Now Rick was stuck—he had to ask her to dance. Stephanie wished she'd never come to this dumb event.

"Now that I've found you," said Rick cheerfully, "would you like to dance?"

"Uh . . . I was just about to leave," Stephanie replied in a small voice. "I've got to look over some chemistry notes before next period."

"Ah, come on, Steph, you've got plenty of time for that. Just one dance." He put his hand firmly on her arm. Stephanie could feel his warmth . . . and determination. Her blood raced madly. He really did want to dance with her!

"Sure . . . okay," she said shyly.

"I've been looking for you for half an hour," Rick confessed, leading her onto the dance floor and putting his arms around her. "Where were you? I thought you'd stood me up."

"I . . . uh . . . no," she stuttered, trying to organize her thoughts. But being so close to him like this unnerved her completely.

Slowly and gently Rick pulled her to his chest and started to dance. Stephanie's heart pounded as a flood of sensations rippled through her. Their bodies were touching and the air suddenly seemed thick and close and much too warm. Her pleasure was so acute, it was almost painful. She tried to pull back, but Rick held her fast. Her mind whirled in confusion. Her own feelings were racing out of control and she didn't want to let that happen. Stephanie could feel her hands getting sweaty.

"Were you really looking for me, or did Alex drag you over?" Stephanie asked. Her voice sounded as though it came from far away, like the DJ's voice announcing the records from the other end of the gym.

"What do you think?" Rick whispered in her ear, wrapping her even closer in his arms.

"I just wanted to be sure."

"I was looking for you when I came across Alex who was also looking for you, so we combined our genius and . . . ta . . . daaaaaaaa, it worked!"

Stephanie laughed at his antics, then hugged him lightly. Suddenly everything made sense. All at once the world was a pretty amazing place. She sighed softly and rested her head on Rick's shoulder.

The records boomed out their message in the background, but the only message Stephanie heard was the pounding of her heart and the feeling that Rick wanted her here in his arms.

The minutes ticked off slowly, and a new song began. But Stephanie was oblivious of it all, and of the familiar faces that floated by. She was lost in the world she and Rick had created around themselves, of feeling his warm, secure arms around her, of breathing in his clean, soapy smell. They danced every song, even the intervals between, never breaking their own slow beat.

"Okay, you guys," Marcia Connors announced from the stage when the music finally stopped. Her rich, low voice oozed out over the microphone.

Everyone stopped dancing. Stephanie stared at her in awe. She'd never known anyone quite as perfect-looking as Marcia, except maybe in the magazines. Her dark brown hair tumbled in thick, luxurious waves around her perfectly shaped face and large, liquid-brown eyes. Her bold, Brooke Shields face made Stephanie doubly insecure of her own delicate features. Why would someone like Rick, one of the wealthiest, most popular boys in school, be interested in her when he could easily have someone like Marcia? In fact, from what she'd heard, Marcia would be more than willing to start something with Rick. Stephanie shuddered at the possibility.

"That's it for this week," said Marcia, flashing her million-dollar smile. "Remember, the Pep Squad made it all happen here, so you come out and support us. Okay?"

Everyone clapped and stomped, then filed out of the gym. Rick kept her hand in his as they wove in and out of the crowd. Stephanie spotted Alex not far off.

"Alex, what time did you say that swim meet was?" called Stephanie.

"Three-thirty."

"I'll be there, so you better do some hot stuff diving, okay?"

"You bet!" shouted Alex, grinning broadly before disappearing into the crowd.

Rick walked her to class. It was the first time he'd done this, and Stephanie tried to figure out if it was just her imagination, or if the other kids were really looking at her differently—as if she were one of them, and no longer an outsider.

"Stephanie, if you aren't doing anything tomorrow, would you like to hang out at my house?" asked Rick when they paused outside her classroom. "Maybe play some tennis, go for a swim. Stuff like that."

Stephanie's heart soared with a feeling of joy and then fear. He was asking her out! On a real date! But to his house, one of the biggest in Glenwood, with its own pool and tennis courts. She didn't even know how to play tennis. But she wasn't going to give up this chance of being with Rick. No way.

"Sure," she said with false confidence. "Sounds like fun."

"Great, I'll pick you up around ten. That okay?"

Stephanie floated through the rest of the day. She had a date! She was just like the other kids, getting excited about the weekend, looking forward to going out with someone she really cared for. It was wonderful. When the final bell of the day rang, she grabbed her books and headed for the pool. She couldn't wait to root for Glenwood. Her school! And her sister was the star diver!

"Hey, babe, wanna roll out to Stillwell Beach and drink a few beers?"

Stephanie spun around and found herself staring up through a tumble of dark, unruly hair into the deep-set, black eyes of Kirk Wallace. She sucked in her breath and involuntarily took a step back. Kirk's shirt was unbuttoned halfway, revealing a V of lean but powerful chest. As he stepped in beside her, his movements sleek and catlike, he exuded a kind of fascinating but deadly charm. Stephanie always thought he'd make a great athlete if he'd ever try out for a team, but he considered anything to do with high school completely beneath him. Most of his time was spent working on cars or running around with his gang of tough friends.

Stephanie's heart skipped a beat. Why did he have to pick now of all times to hassle her? She glanced quickly around, hoping none of her friends could see her. She knew how much they disapproved of Kirk, even though they'd all finally admitted that he was one of the sexiest guys at Glenwood in a scary sort of way.

"Nah, I'm going to the swim meet," said Stephanie lightly, hoping he'd take the hint and bug off.

"Well, la tee daaa. Next we'll be trying out for the cheerleading squad," Kirk said sarcastically. "Since when have we become so concerned about our dear old school?"

"Come on, Kirk, give me a break," Stephanie pleaded. "Alex is diving today. I want to see how she does."

"Ho, ho! You really are becoming part of the in crowd around this place, aren't you?" he said, gripping her arm tightly. "What's the matter? Your old friends not good enough for you anymore, huh?"

"Get your hands off me, Kirk Wallace!" cried Stephanie angrily. "Leave me alone." Stephanie tried to wrench her arm free, but he squeezed tighter. Tears of pain stood out in her large coppery eyes.

"Hey, that's pretty tough talk for a jailbird, don't you think?" His dark eyes flashed menacing sparks.

Stephanie's insides froze. "Ha! You don't know what you're talking about," she bluffed.

"Kirk Wallace always knows what he's talking about," he growled back. "Unfortunately for you, my good buddy, Bruiser, was checked into the County Jail Hilton the same time you were last year. Now isn't that an interesting little fact?"

Stephanie swallowed hard, her mind racing. She'd only been behind bars for the weekend. Actually she'd only been booked for a night, but her foster family made her stay for the entire weekend to teach her a lesson. Well, she'd learned two lessons: how to hot wire a car, and how to pick a lock in three seconds flat. That was some exchange for stealing a lousy pack of smokes, she thought bitterly.

"Come on, kid, I think we have a lot to talk about," said Kirk, dragging her roughly over to his low-rider Camaro. It was purple and black; Stephanie hated the car, but she was terrified enough to obey. Kirk was one tough character. Somehow she had to talk some sense into him. If he started spreading rumors around about her past, everything would be ruined. Everything.

Kirk spun out of the school parking lot, leaving a patch of smoking rubber, and headed for the coast road, steering with one hand and drinking a beer with the other.

"That Forrester kid's no good for ya, babe. He's not your type," he said.

"How about letting me decide?" retorted Stephanie.

Kirk laughed. "Since you've done so well with the rest of your life, why not?" He ran his beer can down her bare arm. Stephanie shrank back. "That guy doesn't know how to love a real woman." He leered.

"And I suppose you do," she snarled. She had to show this jerk she wasn't scared of him, beat him at his own game.

"Try me."

"Ha! Not a chance, cowboy. Rick and I are tight."

"I guess we could find out how tight by telling him his innocent-looking girl friend is really a jailbird, huh?"

Stephanie stared down at her nails. For the first time in her life they weren't bitten down to the skin. It was so nice to have real fingernails. Lori had shown her how to manicure them. And she was just getting up the nerve to buy some fire engine red polish.

"Kirk," she said, her voice small and pleading, "please don't start blabbing about my past around school. It would ruin everything. Please."

When Kirk didn't immediately reply, Stephanie

glanced at him from the corner of her eye. His face was dark and brooding, but not so fierce. He almost looked normal. Maybe she'd finally reached him.

"I bet it would," he said, turning to her. "So what do I get if I keep my mouth shut?"

Stephanie looked at him helplessly. "I don't know. I don't have much to offer."

"You got plenty, in my book," he said with a chuckle that sent spasms of fear down her back. She couldn't believe she'd actually gone out with this guy before. Those days seemed so far in the past. Almost like another lifetime.

There was silence for a moment. Stephanie didn't know what to say. What could she say? He held all the cards.

"Hey . . . look, kid," Kirk said, his voice suddenly soft. "I guess what I'm trying to say is you and I are two of a kind. We like our freedom. We don't play anyone else's games — Forrester's from a different world. His old man is a bigwig. They're loaded. Rick's never going to understand you, and you're never going to understand him. Why make yourself miserable? I have much more to offer you."

Stephanie already felt miserable. Much as she wanted to deny what Kirk was saying, there was a lot of truth in it. How long could she go on deceiving Rick? Already she'd told him she was Alex's cousin and was just staying with Alex's family until her mother got back from Europe. How many of these lies could she make up? At least with Kirk she'd have nothing to hide.

She glanced at the clock on the dash and when she saw the time, a wave of nausea hit her. It was three-thirty; the diving meet was starting. Alex would be looking for her. What was she going to think when Stephanie didn't show? Frustration knotted her stomach and gnawed away at her insides. Things were just starting to get really good between her and Alex. This could blow their whole relationship.

As the speedometer climbed, she clutched the seat, her knuckles growing white. Why did Kirk have to drive so fast? she wondered. He seemed so self-destructive sometimes. What was he trying to prove?

Finally, Kirk swung off the main road onto a sandy track that dead-ended at Stillwell Beach. The last time Stephanie had been here, she'd been with the gang and Gayle Rogers. They'd been celebrating Gayle's victory over her weight. She'd reached her goal of 115 pounds—60 pounds lighter than she had been. They'd thrown the Frisbee and swum and eaten tons of carrot sticks and sliced apples and joked about how much they hated carrot sticks and sliced apples, then gone back to town for a pizza. It had been a great day.

Now the beach was taken over by fifteen or twenty really tough-looking kids. One bunch was roaring around in their low-riders tearing up huge sections of the beach and laughing drunkenly at the destruction. Others were sitting on their cars watching the show and throwing beer cans in the paths of the racing tires. From somewhere, ear-splitting, heavy metal music drowned out the crash of the waves and the cries of protest from the sea gulls.

"Hey...ever see these?" said Kirk, sliding his car

to a halt. He pulled up the sleeve of his shirt. Two tattoos stood out on his muscular arm. Stephanie stared in disgust. One was a naked lady. Underneath was written, "Brenda." The other showed a heart with a dagger through it.

"Know what this means?" asked Kirk, his lips curling over his teeth in a wicked grin as he pointed to the dagger.

Stephanie shook her head. She was in a daze. This whole scene was a nightmare.

"It means, 'don't mess with me.'" He grabbed her arm and pulled her from the car. "So, don't mess with me, okay? Let's have fun." He dragged her over to the crowd.

"Kirk, my man, where'd you get the foxy chick?" yelled a beefy-looking guy.

"At a spelling bee," retorted Kirk, accepting a beer from an outstretched hand. Everyone roared with laughter. Stephanie's cheeks burned.

While Kirk got into the action, Stephanie shrank into the background. Once it was established she was "Kirk's girl," no one bothered her. Slowly her heartbeat returned to normal, but the scene before her continued to disgust her. Kirk was obviously a leader, although he seemed to stay more on the sidelines egging the others on in their craziness instead of joining in himself. They were all dancing now, kicking sand over each other in their wild frenzy and spilling beer all over the place.

Suddenly Stephanie realized she was seeing herself the way she used to be; she recognized the same false bravado and devil-may-care reckless, insensitive, and selfish attitude. It didn't matter to her that in the past people had treated her callously and sometimes cruelly—she didn't allow herself the luxury of that excuse. Her loathing turned inward, and a tear slid down her cheek, as she felt her whole body sag in remorse.

Kirk was right. She really was unworthy of Rick.

Chapter Two

Stephanie woke slowly the next morning. She opened one eye, then the other, wishing for all the world that she could just roll over and go back to sleep. But the sun poured through the windows, dappling the walls and glinting off Noodle's trophy. It was a beautiful day, begging her to get up and join in. Stephanie sighed and rolled on her back, the nightmare of last night flooding back. She didn't know what time she'd gotten in, but she knew it was late. Everyone at the Enomoto house had been asleep.

"Steph . . . you awake?"

Stephanie tensed. *Uh-oh,* she thought, *here comes Alex to give me a hard time about missing the meet* and *not calling to say where I was.* Stephanie shrank down in the covers. Maybe if she was real quiet Alex would think she was asleep and go away.

"Steph, it's nine o'clock," came Alex's voice on the other side of the door. "Isn't Rick picking you up at ten?"

Stephanie sat up with a jolt. She'd almost forgotten the note she'd slipped Alex in English class yesterday telling her about the date with Rick. She'd been so excited and happy, she had to share it with someone. Now she wished Rick had never asked her out.

"Yeah, I'm awake," said Stephanie, still praying that Alex would go away and leave her alone. She wasn't in the mood to apologize to anyone for anything.

"Thought you would be," Alex said, walking in, a steaming cup of tea in hand. "Here, I figured you could use this."

Stephanie took it warily. "Thanks," she mumbled.

"So, did you have a good time last night?" asked Alex, plopping down on the foot of the bed.

Here it comes, thought Stephanie. *The Grand Inquisition.* "Yeah, it was okay."

"I guess I just got kind of worried when you weren't in by midnight," said Alex.

"I don't need you to worry about me," Stephanie snapped.

"I know. I just wanted to be sure you were okay."

"I've told you before . . . I'm old enough to look after myself." Stephanie shifted her weight, and a dull pain shot through her arm. Looking down, she saw a black-and-blue swelling where Kirk had held her so tightly. Quickly she pulled the bedcovers up over it.

"Well," said Alex, getting up and walking to the

door, a hurt look on her face, "as long as you're okay. That's all I came in for."

Stephanie was torn. Alex hadn't come in to give her a rough time after all. She was really concerned. If only Stephanie could bring herself to tell Alex about last night. A lump rose in her throat.

"Alex..." began Stephanie. Alex stuck her head back in the door.

"Yes?"

"How'd the meet go?"

"Great! We won!"

"I'm sorry I wasn't there," said Stephanie.

"Ah...don't worry about it. There're plenty of others."

"I'll be at the next one...I promise."

Alex smiled, and as she closed the door behind her, Stephanie called out softly, "Thanks for the tea, Alex. It's really good."

Rick's red Ferrari hummed up the long, winding driveway. As she watched the evenly spaced, ancient eucalyptus trees flash by on either side, Stephanie's stomach churned.

"We're going to have a great day," announced Rick enthusiastically, slipping smoothly into second gear to take the sharp curve at the top. "Mom and Dad are looking forward to meeting you."

Stephanie was silent. She wasn't sure what this day might bring, but she did know she was about to enter a foreign world. Could she handle it?

The car swung under an arch into a stone courtyard. Stephanie sucked in her breath, her last bit of confidence instantly fleeing. The house before her was even more incredible than she'd imagined. It was huge, built in the old Spanish hacienda style with white adobe walls, wrought-iron balconies around each window, and wide, tiled porches. Large urns were filled with masses of colorful flowers that swayed gently in the breeze like ladies in beautiful summer dresses.

"My grandfather built it," said Rick. "He was one of the original forty-niners in the California gold rush. A real character, from all reports. We have some of his old diaries and logbooks in the library."

Rick helped her from the car and led her through another arch into an interior courtyard. It was long and rectangular, covered entirely in broad, terra-cotta tiles, except for the pool that shimmered invitingly in the middle. Graceful arches led away from the courtyard across porches to the living quarters beyond. At the juncture of the arches, heavy black iron lamps stood out in stark contrast to the startling white walls. Clusters of white wicker furniture were scattered here and there ready to receive the rich and famous. At least that's what it seemed like to Stephanie.

She stared, trying to take it all in. There was a quiet, cool, expensive hush to the place. Even the birds seemed to sing more sweetly here, and under one of the many potted palms that were dotted about sat a sassy parrot, decked out in feathers of blue and red and yellow. It eyed her suspiciously from its rattan perch.

A door slid open from across the way, and Mr. and Mrs. Forrester moved slowly and elegantly into view. At least Stephanie assumed this handsome couple were Rick's parents. They had Rick's same tall, slender, athletic grace. Mrs. Forrester seemed to float toward them on the soft folds of her sea green caftan, and in his tennis whites and deep tan, Mr. Forrester looked surprisingly young.

"And so, Stephanie," said Mrs. Forrester when they'd all been introduced and were seated at a poolside table. A large, striped umbrella shielded them from the sun. "Richard tells me your mother is an opera singer. How thrilling."

It took Stephanie several seconds to realize that Richard was "Rick." No one at school called him Richard.

"Yes," said Stephanie, trying desperately to keep her cool. "She has a beautiful voice." For all she knew her mother really was an opera singer. The only memory she had of her mother was sitting on her lap listening to the most beautiful songs in the world.

"Our daughter Isabelle wanted a singing career, too," broke in Mr. Forrester, "but she ended up going into computers instead. Isn't that a curious turnabout?"

Stephanie smiled and nodded. Rick's parents really were imposing-looking, and she knew they had superimpressive careers. Mrs. Forrester was a consultant for Abacus, one of the most famous West Coast fashion houses. Mr. Forrester was an ex-tennis pro who now flew all over the country giving clinics to the rich and famous. But they seemed really nice, too. Stephanie allowed herself to relax a little.

"Actually, Isabelle is an electrical design engineer," added Mrs. Forrester. "In Silicon Valley. We're very proud of her, aren't we, dear?" She reached over and clasped Mr. Forrester's hand. He smiled tenderly back at her.

"Yes, Isabelle's come a long, long way," sighed Mrs. Forrester, her voice trailing off. She fidgeted absentmindedly with the heavy jeweled rings on her long, slender fingers.

Stephanie wondered what they meant by "a long, long way." Probably all the schooling she'd been through. It must take a lot of hard work to be a design engineer. Obviously Isabelle was yet another success story in the Forrester family history.

"And," added Mrs. Forrester excitedly, "she's getting married. Later this month. Right here by the pool."

Again Stephanie smiled. "What a perfect place for a wedding," she said. "Where are they going on their honeymoon?"

"Tahiti, the lucky devils," said Rick. "Can you believe it?"

Stephanie couldn't. She'd never been out of the state.

"That sounds wonderful, very romantic," she said, hoping this was the right response.

"Oh, it is!" sighed Mrs. Forrester. "I was there last spring looking for a new line of materials, and I tell you it was heaven on Earth. Arthur and I plan to go back this fall."

"Wouldn't you know they'd plan it when I was in school," teased Rick, giving Stephanie a mischievous wink.

"Ah, yes," broke in his father, "but don't forget you get all summer in Europe if you graduate in the top five percent of your class."

For a moment, Rick didn't reply, and Stephanie sensed a feeling of tension. Then he grinned sheepishly. "Okay. Okay. When you put it like that, I guess I'll let you go."

Stephanie's head was spinning. Europe! Tahiti! Wow! They talked about going to these places the way she talked about going to the beach for the afternoon. It was incredible. She shot Rick a quick look. He found her hand under the table and squeezed it gently. Shivers ran up and down her spine, and she relaxed again.

"Ah . . . lunch," said Mr. Forrester, moving aside while the Mexican servant put the plates on the table. "This looks wonderful, Juanita. Thank you."

"*Bon appetit,* everyone," Mrs. Forrester said cheerily before starting into her salad.

Stephanie watched Rick out of the corner of her eye. She wasn't even sure what they were eating, much less which knife or fork to use. There was a display of each on either side of her plate. Following his lead, she picked up the smaller fork to the left of her plate.

"I tell you, Juanita makes the best guacamole salad I've ever tasted," murmured Mrs. Forrester, dabbing at the corners of her mouth with the heavy linen table napkin.

So this is guacamole, thought Stephanie. She'd heard of it, but this was the first time she'd actually eaten any. It made her feel very exotic and sophisticated.

Thick, cool gazpacho soup followed, accompanied by a basket of crusty French bread, and again

Stephanie was thrilled to discover a new taste. The meal was unhurried and delicious, ending with a refreshing lemon mousse served in tall parfait glasses. When Juanita had cleared the last dish away, they sat around sipping espresso coffee in dainty china cups and talking. At least Rick and his parents talked. Stephanie just listened, awed by the world they so calmly accepted as normal—jetting off to London or Paris for the weekend, vacationing with people Stephanie only knew from the pages of *People* magazine, and discussing if it made better sense for Rick to go to Harvard or Stanford in the fall.

"Okay, kids, how about a leisurely game of tennis to settle the old tum?" said Mr. Forrester, finally pushing back his chair. "What do you say?"

Stephanie felt the knot return inside. She'd done a good job of faking it so far, but playing tennis was stretching it. She'd never even held a racket.

"You do play, don't you, Stephanie?" asked Mr. Forrester when she hesitated.

"No . . . no, I don't," she replied, her mind racing. "I always moved around so much with my mother, I didn't have a chance to learn."

"Well, no problem," said Mr. Forrester jovially. "I'm supposed to be the expert. I'll have you whacking away in no time." He turned to his son. "Mind if I steal her for a little while?"

Rick laughed. "You've just made my dad's day. He loves a new victim."

Stephanie smiled weakly and let Rick lead her off to the courts behind Mr. Forrester. At least she was dressed for it. Alex had lent her a pair of stylishly baggy white shorts and a lime green tank top. She thought of the shirt she'd borrowed yesterday from Alex. It was hidden in the corner of her room, still reeking of beer from Kirk's wild friends. She hoped it wasn't ruined. The horror of last night came flooding back, and again Stephanie was afraid that she had no place in Rick's world. Everybody was being so nice and open with her, and all she could give them in return were lies.

"Okay, Stephanie," said Mr. Forrester when they'd reached the tennis court, which was surrounded by a flowering hedge. There was a tree-shaded cabana off to one side with white wicker furniture lounging casually inside. Stephanie wished she could escape to its cool interior and watch Rick and his father play. Her knees felt rubbery and completely uncooperative. "Here's your racket," continued Mr. Forrester, coming over to stand beside her. "Grab the end of the handle here as if you were shaking hands with it . . . good, that's it."

The racket, one of the latest, oversized styles, felt heavy and awkward. Stephanie was afraid her wrist would break if she had to hold it very long. She glanced over at Rick sitting on a bench at the side. He grinned at her, and despite her fear, Stephanie grinned back, feeling a little confidence return. After all she'd always been pretty good at sports, what few she'd been forced to play in PE at her various schools. Might as well give tennis her best shot since there seemed to be no way out of it.

"Okay, turn your body sideways to the net and get your racket back in position," shouted Mr. Forrester from the other side of the net, demonstrating what he meant. Stephanie did as she was told, trying to make her body look as loose and relaxed as Mr. Forrester's. He lobbed the first ball slowly over the net.

"Keep your eye on the ball," he called.

Stephanie's eyes strained, watching the small white sphere hit the pinkish court and bounce toward her.

"Move in on it, and swing slowly and evenly," directed Mr. Forrester calmly. "And follow through with your racket in the direction you want the ball to go."

Stephanie doggedly followed his orders.

Thwock. The ball connected with her racket and sailed back over the net. Stephanie stared dumbly after it, then down at her racket.

"Way to go, Steph!" yelled Rick, hooting and clapping.

"Bravo!" shouted Mr. Forrester bounding up to the net and smiling broadly with surprise. "Well done, Stephanie."

Stephanie's cheeks burned. Okay, so she'd had a lucky shot. There was no guarantee she could do it again.

But she did! Ball after ball flew back over the net, each one a little smoother and more controlled than the last. Rick was on his feet now shouting encouragement, and Mr. Forrester was sending the balls over faster and lower. Stephanie felt a new energy flowing through her as she tore around the court. There was a real sense of satisfaction when her racket resounded with that hollow thwock every time she hit the ball dead center.

When the three of them returned to the pool an hour later, Stephanie's cheeks were flushed with excitement.

"She's great!" Mr. Forrester bragged to his wife. "A real natural." He put his arm around Stephanie's shoulders. "I just can't believe you've never played tennis before."

Stephanie's color deepened. She could see Rick and Mrs. Forrester smiling proudly at her. "You're just a great teacher, Mr. Forrester," she said. "Thanks a lot for the lesson."

"Anytime," he replied, "but Rick can teach you as much as I can. He's an ace."

"Or you can sit in the shade and drink lemonade with me," added Mrs. Forrester. "I can't bear the heat."

Everyone laughed.

"And speaking of the heat," said Rick, sliding his arm around Stephanie's waist. "What do you say to a swim?"

"I'd love it," said Stephanie enthusiastically. She wasn't a great swimmer, but that didn't matter. Right now she felt she could take on the world. Even Rick's world. It didn't seem nearly so frightening anymore.

"Well, I think we'll leave you kids to it," said Mr. Forrester, offering his arm to his wife. "Time for a siesta for us old folks."

The one thing Stephanie had bought was a beautiful bathing suit. She'd seen it at the Emporium weeks ago but had only just gotten up the nerve to buy it. Kit had declared it the bathing suit of the century. It was a black one-piece cut up high on the sides to show off her slender legs, and cut low in the front and back.

She slipped into it in the changing room next to the pool, then raced into the water self-consciously to join Rick. She'd never worn anything so revealing before, but the lady in the shop kept insisting she had the perfect body for it.

Rick swam over to her in strong, steady strokes. His eyes looked brilliant in his tanned face. Stephanie smiled. Her bathing suit had made a hit. She could tell. When he stood up, the water rolled off his bronzed chest, and her eyes were drawn to his flat, muscular stomach. In a swift motion he grabbed her arm and pulled her in close. His skin against hers was warm and cool at the same time, and he smelled all fresh and clean.

"Hey, careful there," quipped Stephanie, pulling back, "that's my tennis arm. You don't want to ruin my game, do you?"

"Ah-ha! So now we're the big tennis ace, are we?" shot back Rick, increasing his grip. "Not till you've passed my test, kid."

In the next instant Stephanie was flying through the air. She landed with a loud splash. When she came up, she swam quickly after him, but he took off. Finally, she dived down and tickled his stomach from below. They came up together, laughing and sputtering.

"Tickling's not allowed," said Rick, laughing and shaking the water from his eyes. "That's my weak spot."

"Now I know." Stephanie giggled, lunging after him again and grabbing his sides in her hands. His muscles were firm and taut, his skin smooth. In that moment, she was off guard, lost in the wonderful feeling of his body in her hands, enabling him to spin around and sweep her off her feet. She lay cradled, helplessly, in his arms, their faces inches apart. They stared at each other, their breath coming hard and uneven. Stephanie was painfully aware of the lack of clothing between them, aware of their bodies touching. The water swirled sensuously around them, and she moved her legs slowly against it.

When Rick's lips found hers, Stephanie felt as if she were drowning. Her skin burned where he touched her, while the chill of goose bumps rose all over. Deeper and deeper he explored, drawing Stephanie into a world of sun and skin and wonderful sensations. Her breath burned deep in her chest. Backing up, Rick pulled her through the water until her back touched the edge of the pool. She hesitated, then slowly laced her arms around his neck and held him close, a soft sigh escaping her lips.

Suddenly Stephanie pulled back. Rick's hand was moving higher and higher, exploring forbidden territory.

"Rick, no," she gasped, wiggling to get free. "Please don't."

He moaned and buried his head in her neck.

"You feel so good," he said, his breath coming in rasps.

He probably thinks I'm pretty loose, thought Stephanie, struggling to get her own breathing under control. She'd given a lot of people that impression when she first came to Glenwood with her woman-of-the-world tough act. She shuddered.

"Cold?" he asked tenderly.

Stephanie was taken aback. She'd expected him to be angry at her for stopping his game.

"No...no, I'm not cold," she said. "I just have to get home."

"Oh," he said with disappointment. "I was hoping we could take in a movie or something tonight."

"I'd love to, but I promised Alex I'd be home by five. It's Mrs. Enomoto's—Aunt Susan's—birthday, and they've got a surprise dinner planned."

"Well, it's just past four now, so we'd better hurry." He helped her out of the pool and showed her where the lights were in the changing room.

Stephanie dressed in record time. As much as he'd freaked her out with his come-on, she couldn't bear for them to be apart. The rest of their day had been magic. She felt like a different person. Even her face looked different, she thought, standing in front of the mirror and pulling a comb through her sun-streaked hair. Her cheeks were rosy and not so sunken-looking, and her eyes glowed brightly. She swept her hair back from her face with both hands, then turned her head from side to side to observe the effect. Usually she felt very insecure if she didn't have a curtain of hair to hide behind, but right now she liked it. Her eyes seemed even bigger, and her cheekbones more prominent. The gang was always telling her what great cheekbones she had. Why not show them? Maybe she'd start wearing her hair like Elaine's—pulled back at either side of her head with snappy clips, or tortoiseshell combs for a more sophisticated look.

She quickly applied a layer of shell pink lipstick

and smacked her lips together as she'd seen Lori do. Her mouth would never be the perfect bow shape of Kit's, but it was full and expressive. It was okay. In fact, everything about the way she looked was okay today. For once she didn't have a million complaints.

"Wow!" Rick exclaimed. "That was fast! You're the first girl I ever knew who didn't stay in a bathroom half the night doing whatever it is girls do in there." He took her hand. "Plus, you look great."

Stephanie blushed. Rick was so open and direct. She liked it, but sometimes it took her off guard. So many people in her life had been two-faced and sneaky.

"You must be freezing, though," he said, looking up at the newly arrived clouds and putting his arm around her bare shoulders. "Let me get you something." He was back in two minutes with a beautiful white cashmere sweater. Its soft luxury floated around her slender body. It was way too big, coming almost down to the end of her shorts, but Stephanie loved it. It smelled like Rick and was warm and cuddly. She shivered with happiness while he rolled the sleeves back over her small wrists.

The eucalyptus trees were silhouetted hulks swaying gently to and fro as the car slid easily down the drive. The valleys were deep in shade, though the tops of the hills were still bathed in golden light.

"I had a wonderful day, Rick," said Stephanie, smiling sleepily over at him. "Thank you so much."

His smile set her heart beating out of control again. "I had a wonderful day, too, Steph." He reached over and took her hand in his. "I hope I didn't take things too fast." He paused. "You know what I mean. I wouldn't want to hurt you for anything in the world."

Stephanie dropped her head so her hair covered her scarlet cheeks. Shyly she shook her head. Although she was sure no one at Glenwood High would believe it, she didn't know much about sex. When she'd first arrived at GHS, she'd worked so hard to come across as the devil-may-care renegade, running around with Kirk Wallace and his wild crowd, that most people had come to believe she was pretty experienced. Actually, it was embarrassing how little she knew. No one had ever taken the time to sit down and discuss sex with her. They seemed to assume she knew all about it . . . firsthand.

She knew Kit went to bed with Justin and that Danny and Alex had made love, too, but she'd never gotten the nerve up to ask them about it. And her last foster sister's pregnancy had been a nightmare. Paula's parents had yelled at Stephanie for leading their daughter astray, then forced Paula to have an abortion. Paula had gone really weird after that, and Stephanie had been sent back to Crestview Home for Girls, where the Enomotos found her.

"You know, Steph," said Rick, his voice coming from miles away and snapping Stephanie back to the present. "You're not like other girls. I can really have fun with you. I like that."

Stephanie shrank at his words. One thing she'd loved about the day with Rick was feeling so normal; of being just like any other seventeen-year-old girl out on a Saturday having a good time with her boyfriend. Rick's words reminded her how false this illusion was. If only he knew how unlike other girls she really was.

"No, it's true," he continued, misinterpreting her silence. "I've really had a great time today. It's nice to meet someone who's not afraid to try new things—I mean, you were incredible on the tennis courts—and isn't all worried about getting her hair wet. Stuff like that. So many girls seem more concerned about their makeup running than just relaxing and having fun. You're a real free spirit, and that's refreshing. I admire that." Rick hesitated, then put his arm around her shoulders.

Stephanie didn't know what to say. She couldn't deny his words thrilled her, but what would he say if she told him she'd been lying to him about her past? Would he think she was so much fun? Would he admire her then?

"Rick, watch out!" Stephanie cried suddenly.

Rick slammed on the brakes and slid to a halt. A tiny kitten swayed unsteadily on its matchstick legs in the middle of the road. Rick honked the horn, but the kitten just stood there.

"Oh, Rick, the poor little thing," Stephanie cried, leaping from the car. "It's so skinny."

Stephanie scooped the scrawny orange animal up in her arms and held it close. It was so thin, its eyes seemed to take up its entire face. It meowed softly and licked her hand with its rough, dry tongue.

"Someone probably didn't want it and threw it out," said Rick. "It happens all the time out here."

"How could they?" demanded Stephanie, outraged. "It's so little and helpless. It could die."

"That's what they hope will happen."

"Well, I think that's wicked. I'm going to take it

home and look after it," she declared, kissing the matted hair on the top of its head. "It needs to be loved, too."

Rick helped her get settled back in the car with the kitten on her lap. It lay limp, panting hard.

"I think it's thirsty," said Rick. "There's a creek at the bottom of the hill. We can get it some water there."

He pulled over beside the tumbling brook and brought back some water to the kitten in a tennis ball can. It lapped the water up eagerly, and Rick had to go back twice more before the kitten seemed satisfied.

"Poor kitty," said Rick tenderly, stroking its soft baby fur. "I don't know how people can treat animals like this. They don't want it, so they toss it out. They never think of the suffering the poor animal will go through." Suddenly he gave Stephanie a mischievous grin and bent over the kitten's ear. "Gazpacho, you are one lucky cat, I tell you, to be going home with Miss Stephanie Burroughs. You better share her, though, 'cause I want to spend a lot of time with her, too. Okay?"

Stephanie laughed, though her face flushed from his obvious compliment. "Gazpacho! You're going to call this poor thing Gazpacho?"

"Can you think of a better name?" asked Rick, trying to look hurt.

Stephanie leaned over and kissed his cheek. "No . . . I can't. I think it's a perfect name." She turned to the cat, who was purring away in her lap. "But Gazpacho, if this guy doesn't get me home pronto, I'm going to be in mucho trouble."

Rich laughed and swung the car back onto the road.

Later that night Stephanie lay in bed trying to get to sleep, but images from the day filled her mind to overflowing: the amazing house, the closeness and warmth of Rick's family, the satisfaction of finally hitting a tennis ball properly, the feel of Rick's skin against hers, the cool water wrapping itself around their warm bodies, his arms, his smile, their kiss. It had been absolutely the best day ever.

But it wasn't her world. Not by a long shot. When she and Rick were together, it didn't seem to matter. Her happiness made her forget reality. But, from afar, the reality was too brutal to deny. All the lies she'd told him made her feel sick, but what could she do? She certainly couldn't tell him the truth. To people like the Forresters you just didn't admit you had no idea who your father was or that your mother gave you away. Sure, they were friendly and pretty openminded, but in their world there were some things that just weren't acceptable. Rick *thought* he was in love with her now, but would he still be if he learned about the real Stephanie? Nothing in his world had prepared him to deal with problems such as hers. He would try, of course, but sooner or later, Rick would realize that it couldn't work out. It would be the end.

Gazpacho shifted his weight beside her and settled down once again. He'd eaten so much dinner, Stephanie was a little worried for him. She couldn't imagine where his tiny body was putting it all. The whole family had gathered around in amazement,

Mrs. Enomoto's birthday celebration almost forgotten in the excitement of welcoming the new member into the family.

Stephanie reached down and scratched his head. She felt very close to this small, orange fuzz-ball. They had a lot in common. They were orphans, dumped at the mercy of the world. But had her mother really tossed her out like some unwanted kitten? Could she have meant so little to her mother? Had her mother ever loved her? A hollow opened up in the pit of Stephanie's stomach. If only she could sit down, just once, and talk things over with her mother, maybe she wouldn't feel so empty.

Rick knew all about his family history. If only she could find out about hers—who her parents were, and her grandparents, too. That would explain so much. Then maybe she could begin to really understand herself, then she'd feel free to open up to Rick, to pursue a relationship with him. She wasn't sure at this point what a romantic relationship was supposed to involve.

Stephanie's stomach churned. Keeping so much inside hurt. Suddenly, she sat up. Wait a minute! Wasn't this what a mother was for—to help daughters answer all the bewildering, crazy questions? Stephanie struck her pillow with her fist. Well then, she'd just have to find her mother. It was time to go for it. Stephanie needed her now. A rush of energy pulsed through her body, but seconds later, she was lost in a deep, dreamless sleep.

Chapter Three

Stephanie glanced hurriedly up and down the hall. No one in sight. Good. She didn't want anyone around when she made this call. She'd managed to convince Mrs. Casteneda that she had a headache to get out of class a little early. Well, her head really did hurt. She'd agonized all day yesterday whether or not to make this call. Even now she wasn't sure, but Monday was as good a day as any to start a new era in her life.

She slipped the dime into the pay phone by the lunchroom and dialed the number she'd hidden in her purse over a month ago. She'd tried to call from the Enomotos' yesterday—the ad mentioned a twenty-four-hour hotline—but Alex had walked in so she'd hung up.

"Hello," she said when a kindly voice answered. Her heart pounded wildly and her knees threatened to buckle under her.

"Yes...uh...I was just wondering. Isn't this the place that helps kids find their parents?" Her words came out with a rush.

"Well...uh, I'd like to come in and talk to someone please...as soon as possible."

By the time she hung up she had an appointment for that very afternoon after school. Weak with relief and apprehension, she sagged against the wall. She fingered the second dime in her pocket. Maybe she was doing the wrong thing. Maybe her mother didn't want to be found. Maybe she should call back and tell them to forget it. But she hadn't given her name. If she didn't show...well, she didn't show. She could decide later.

"Hi, good-looking."

Stephanie whirled around. The bell had rung without her noticing, and students were starting to pour into the halls. As it wasn't lunchtime, her end of the hall was deserted. Almost. Derek Johnson was leaning against the wall about a foot away with a sleepy look on his face. Stephanie took a step back. She'd heard about his reputation. Kit told her. Derek's game was to get a girl in bed as fast as possible, then brag about it.

"Wanna come over to my house tonight and watch TV with me? Michael Jackson's on...and my parents will be out." He smiled seductively.

Stephanie tried to look bored by his suggestion. She knew it was her fault he was coming on like this—her old reputation coming back to haunt her.

When were people going to notice she'd really changed since her early days at Glenwood? These days she felt as if she were trying on different personalities to see which fit, the way some girls tried on outfits during their weekend shopping sprees.

"No thanks, Derek. I'm not much of a Jackson fan," she said, starting to walk away.

"Then come over anyway and we'll make our own action." Derek laughed.

"I said no and I mean it," Stephanie said, her voice rising in frustration.

"You're passing up a good time," he said, running his finger down her arm.

"Buzz off, Johnson," snapped Stephanie, yanking herself free.

"This punk bothering you, kid?" Kirk stepped up behind Derek and got him in a head hold.

"Naw," said Stephanie. "I took care of it." She looked around nervously. One thing she didn't want was trouble, but somehow she seemed to spell trouble. She always had. "Let him go, Kirk."

"Not before I get an apology out of him," growled Kirk, his eyes glowing with menace.

Derek brought his elbow back into Kirk's stomach. Kirk groaned and lost his hold. Before Stephanie could stop them, they were on the floor bashing away at each other. Then she saw a flick of metal. Kirk had a knife, a dangerous-looking switchblade.

"Kirk! No!" she yelled. "Stop it! Right now!" She could hear the hysteria in her voice.

"Okay, boys, into my office," called Mr. Gonzalez, the principal, running quickly down the hall toward them. "We don't solve problems by fighting in this school."

As Kirk passed her, he slipped her the knife. Stephanie felt its cold metal against her hand.

"Hide this for me... please," begged Kirk in a hoarse whisper. His dark eyes were wide and pleading. There was nothing of the macho man about him now.

Stephanie stared at the knife in disbelief for a second, then dropped it quickly into her rucksack. It would be all over if she got caught with this. Her mind raced, trying to think of somewhere to hide it. Finally, she decided on her locker. She hurried down the hall and slid the knife way into the back of the top shelf in her locker.

Stephanie rushed out to the quad at lunch, eager to find Rick and get lost in his warm, secure world. The scene with Derek and Kirk had really shaken her.

Finally, she saw him sitting under the big eucalyptus tree that had a record of all the lovers of Glenwood High, past and present, carved in its aged bark. The sun danced through his dark curls, and his skin glowed with the vigor of his outdoor life.

Stephanie pulled up short when she got closer. Marcia Connors was sitting beside him looking super cool in baggy yellow coveralls and a funky striped T-shirt. The latest fashion... as usual. Stephanie was still too far away to hear what they were saying, but Marcia was laughing animatedly, and at one point she leaned over and brushed a curl out of Rick's eye. Their easy familiarity tore at Stephanie's soul.

So what, she told herself. *Rick's allowed to have friends.* Maybe that's all it was...friends. If only it weren't Marcia, though. Stephanie didn't trust her at all. Finally, with a toss of her heavy mane, Marcia sauntered off, still laughing at Rick over her shoulder.

"Hi," said Stephanie, approaching him nervously.

His eyes lit up in welcome and he immediately pulled her down beside him.

"Hi...I missed you," he said.

"I missed you, too," she said, her cheeks turning bright pink. *See, he really does care.*

They sat across from each other, straddling the bench, their lunch between them. Rick had a tuna sandwich, and Stephanie had picked up a salad. She dug in hungrily.

"So how's the little orphan?" asked Rick between bites.

Stephanie's fork paused midair. The blood drained from her face. What was he saying?

"Does he like his name?"

Stephanie's breath came out in a rush. Gazpacho! She almost laughed out loud with relief.

"Let's just say he's made himself right at home. He spent most of yesterday asleep in Uncle Bob's leather recliner; the big fancy one he got from that Danish import store in San Francisco. And nobody...I mean *nobody* sits in that chair but Uncle Bob."

"Except..." Rick laughed. "Mighty Gazpacho, the one-pound fearless lion!"

Stephanie giggled. "That's for sure. Uncle Bob didn't even move him. He sat in another chair ordering us all to tiptoe around so we didn't wake the cat!

Can you believe it?"

They both cracked up.

"Hey, you know, you really impressed my dad with your tennis," said Rick.

"I think it's stretching it to call my efforts 'tennis,'" replied Stephanie. "Let's just say I didn't fall flat on my face."

"You're doing it again," chided Rick.

"What?"

"Putting yourself down," Rick said. "I don't know why you do it, but I'm either going to find out, or make you stop—whichever comes first. Now just sit back and accept what I'm saying."

Blood rushed to Stephanie's face. "Okay," she said, leaning back against the tree. "Shoot. Tell me how wonderful I am. I promise not to argue."

"Well, my dad's taught a lot of people to play tennis, and he said you were one of the most impressive beginners he's ever come across. He said you really should take it up seriously."

Stephanie blushed again. She didn't know how to take all these compliments. It was too much. But at the same time, her battered ego swelled with pride.

"Maybe I will," she said, her heart pounding with uncertainty. What if she'd just had a lucky day yesterday? What if she tried again and failed? Her insides twisted at the thought.

"Mr. Emerson, the PE teacher, offers a class for beginners after school on Mondays. Why don't you check it out today?"

"Oh . . . I can't."

"Sure you can. I'll walk you over on my way to tennis practice."

"No, Rick," she said more firmly, terrified that he might pry the truth out about her afternoon plans. "I can't today. I just can't. Okay?"

He shrugged his shoulders and looked bewildered. "Sure, anything you say, but I think you're letting a good opportunity go by."

More than anything Stephanie wanted to level with him, but she just couldn't. Something inside held her back. "So did you and your dad spend the whole day talking about my future as a tennis ace?" she joked, trying to change the subject.

Rick rolled his eyes. "I wish. But you wouldn't believe what we did instead. Mother had Dad and me sitting at the dining room table practically all day taking orders for Isabelle's wedding. You'd think Mother was getting married herself."

"Yeah, she was pretty excited about it all on Saturday, too."

Stephanie was surprised to see Rick go instantly serious. "This wedding means a lot to Mom . . . and Dad, too," he said. "I'm so pleased for them things turned out like this."

Stephanie wanted to ask him to explain what he meant, but he had such a faraway look in his eye, she didn't feel the time was right.

"So how many millions of people are coming?" she asked lightly.

Rick groaned. "At least half the population of northern California, plus some. People will be flying in from all over the world. It's going to be wild."

Stephanie swallowed hard. "Whew, that sounds pretty heavy duty."

"And, the guest list is not even half of it. Mother's

pulling out all the stops for entertainment as well. She's like a mini-mafia going to collect favors from all her old friends."

Stephanie giggled.

"No, I'm serious. Wait'll you hear this. The musicians playing at the wedding are coming from the San Francisco Philharmonic!"

"Wow! How did she manage that?" Stephanie's eyes were opened wide in amazement.

"Some guy she went to school with a million years ago plays cello with them. She helped his daughter get started in design, so I guess he felt obligated to scrounge up some friends to help Mom out."

"Why didn't she just book the Rolling Stones while she was at it?" quipped Stephanie.

"Don't laugh," Rick said, leaning toward her. "She thought about it. The Rolling Stones are Isabelle's favorite group, but they're on tour and weren't available for hire."

Stephanie's head was spinning. "I guess Gennaro's won't be catering the meal, huh?"

Rick laughed. "Well, that was my idea. You know, order a thousand pizzas with everything, keep the money in the neighborhood. I think that's when Mom threw her pen at me . . . or was it her glasses? I tell you, Dad and I were brutalized."

"Poor thing," teased Stephanie, ruffling his hair. "So much suffering."

Reaching out with his strong hands, Rick pulled her to his chest and began showering her with tiny kisses.

"Stop," Stephanie said laughing, trying halfheartedly to pull away. "Stop! You're smothering me!"

"That's the idea," Rick said dramatically, holding her tighter and drowning her in kisses all over her face and neck and hair. "Old Chinese torture. Turns woman to mush."

"Not this 'woman.'" Stephanie giggled. Her body tingled, and her pounding blood made a roaring sound in her ears. She wrapped her arms slowly around Rick's waist. "I guess I'll just have to fight back," she whispered.

Suddenly there was no more play. When Rick's mouth found hers, Stephanie was ready. Happiness at his devious desire, his need for her, swept through her. Folding herself into Rick's arms, Stephanie kissed him back hungrily. Quickly, the shouts, students, the school grounds around them ceased to exist, replaced by a magic wood where she and Rick were alone. A place outside of space and time, where they were free to be together, to love each other . . . unconditionally.

As Stephanie sank further into the intensity of their kiss, she felt strange new feelings stir within her. Suddenly she saw how easy it might be to get carried away, go further than you ever thought you would. Where was she supposed to draw the line? When was she supposed to say no?

Stephanie shuddered involuntarily. All at once she saw her foster father coming at her, the one she'd lived with four years ago. He'd come into her room, his eyes bloodshot and wide with a desire she hadn't understood at first. When he got closer, she could smell the alcohol on his breath and the sweat on his T-shirt. She'd pulled back. At least she thought she had. The memory was so blurred now. She'd forced it into the very back of her mind. She remembered his hairy arms, his dirty fingernails as he'd groped for her. What would have happened if her foster mother hadn't come in just then? Again, a shudder of disgust coursed through Stephanie's thin frame. And the woman had blamed her! How could she blame a thirteen-year-old who was still trying to figure out how to fasten her first bra?

"You okay?" asked Rick, kissing her gently on the forehead. "I felt you pull away."

Stephanie snapped back to the present. The sun shone down brightly on the quad. Kids were walking back and forth, laughing, talking, eating lunch. It was okay. Life was normal now. She was safe. Stephanie smiled up at Rick but she still felt kind of shaky.

"Yeah . . ." she said quietly, putting her head on his shoulder. "Now I'm okay."

"Good, because I have a surprise," he murmured in her ear. "I'm going to immortalize this day, this kiss . . . us . . . on the old eucalyptus tree." He pulled a pocketknife from his jacket. Stephanie gasped out loud as she leaped to her feet.

"Put that thing away," she cried, the horrible scene in the hall that morning still so fresh in her mind.

"Hey . . . all right . . . don't blow a fuse," snapped Rick. "If you don't want our initials up there, just say so. You don't have to flip about it." He snapped the knife closed and put it in his pocket.

"No, Rick, you don't understand," stammered Stephanie. She wanted to explain, but how could she tell him about Derek and Kirk's ugly fight, about Derek's thinking she was easy, about the knife she'd stashed in the back of her locker? Rick's knowing the truth would only open up a can of worms that she wasn't ready to deal with yet.

"Oh, I think I do," he said bitterly. "I'm ready to tell the world about our relationship and you're not. That sums it up, wouldn't you say?" He shook his head in exasperation when she didn't answer. "I just don't understand you, Stephanie. Not at all. I want to. I'm trying very hard to, but sometimes it seems as if you've made up your mind not to let anyone get through to you. And you're proud of it. So what am I supposed to do, huh?"

Stephanie stared at him, her large coppery eyes filling with tears. He stared expectantly back. Suddenly he slammed his fist down on his books.

"Can't you say anything? At least try to help me understand. Or maybe I should start believing the rumors around school that you have something going with Kirk Wallace. Is that what you want me to believe?"

He lifted her face with both his hands so she had to look at him. "Talk to me, Stephanie," he said softly.

Stephanie wrenched her head free. Is that what he thought—that she had the hots for Kirk? She opened her mouth to protest, but nothing came out. Desperately, she tried to remember what she'd told him before. Which of her stories did Rick believe? If she contradicted something she'd said earlier to him, she'd only get herself into more trouble.

"Well, I'd better get to class," he said finally, turning his back on her. "We're certainly not accomplishing anything here. Thanks for lunch."

"Yeah," said Stephanie dismally. "Thanks."

Rick hesitated, then wandered off. Stephanie started after him, then forced herself to stop. Her heart felt as if it were being torn apart with confusion and pain. She stared unseeingly before her, her tears blurring the names on the eucalyptus tree. If only declaring love was as simple as carving initials on a tree, she thought.

Chapter Four

Stephanie checked the address again. Kids Anonymous was in a section of town she'd never been in before. Not that Glenwood had any bad sections, exactly, but this was definitely across the tracks. Typical. No one wanted to know about orphans and foster kids. She'd been walking twenty minutes from school by the time she trudged up the dirty stairs in search of Room 404. No elevator in this building.

She found herself standing before a gray door. KIDS ANONYMOUS the sign said. She stared at it for several moments, her hands clammy, her heart racing. Something about it scared her. What if they actually found her mother? Would she be able to handle it? Her hand shook as she reached for the knob. It turned easily in her hand, and before she realized it, she was inside the room. Stephanie looked across the room and gasped.

Bruce Fletcher! Behind the desk! What was he doing here? Stephanie glanced around in desperation for an escape route. If only the floor would conveniently open up so that she could drop through. No one at school except Alex and the gang knew about her past, but now her cover would be blown. Stephanie didn't know Bruce well, but she'd been around him enough recently to know that he was basically a nice guy. In fact, she and the gang had just finished turning Bruce into a Super Hunk, as they'd jokingly called it. Basically they'd just helped this shy newcomer to feel more comfortable socially at Glenwood. The California high school had been a big change from the all-boys Catholic school he'd attended in Chicago. They'd simply helped Bruce select a more upbeat wardrobe and learn to relax around girls. Stuff like that. Stephanie's job had been to coach him in the art of acting cool. *How appropriate*, she thought, her panic rising. *I wonder how cool I'll seem to him now, when he discovers I'm just a foster kid?* Stephanie swallowed hard, her mind racing.

"Hi, Stephanie, what can I do for you?" asked Bruce, his hazel eyes kind.

"Uh...hi, Bruce. I guess I got the wrong room. This isn't the employment agency, is it?" Stephanie shifted her weight nervously to her other foot.

"No, I'm afraid you missed it by three floors," said Bruce lightly. "But now that you've hauled yourself all the way up here, you might as well have something to drink. Coke or ginger ale?"

"Uh . . . I . . . no," stammered Stephanie.

"No Coke left, so you'll have to have ginger ale," he said, bringing a bottle out of the little refrigerator behind the desk and pouring her a glass.

"That looks good. I might as well join you," he said. "Take a load off your feet. Sit down."

Stephanie sat. He was being so nice, she couldn't refuse. Actually, when she thought about it, she figured she'd learned more from Bruce about how to be a nice person than he'd learned from her about how to be cool. At first, she'd thought he was just naive, then she'd grown to admire the way he always found the good in others. Unlike her, he assumed everyone had some somewhere. Stephanie took a gulp of soda.

"So, what kind of a job are you looking for?" Bruce asked, his feet propped up on the rickety table by the sofa.

"Oh . . . uh . . . anything, really," she lied, nervously twirling the glass in her hands. "I thought it'd be a good idea to make some extra bucks. I might want to go somewhere this summer."

Bruce leaned back on the sofa. He looked really neat in his striped polo shirt and faded jeans—so much better than the old shapeless khaki pants and navy blue school blazers he used to wear. Now you could see what a great body he had. A lot of girls were noticing these days.

"That sounds good," he said, putting his hands behind his head and staring up at the ceiling. "Me, I'd love to take off and hike in the Rockies for a week or two. You know, really get away from it all."

"The Rockies . . . yeah?" said Stephanie, relaxing a

little. "I always wanted to see the Rockies, too. Is that why you're working here?"

"Not really. I don't get paid to do this."

"You don't? What are you doing here, then?" Stephanie asked, almost forgetting what she was doing there. Bruce had a kind of a calming effect on her. Even though they really didn't know each other all that well, he was one of the few people she felt safe around.

"Trying to help people like me," he said, never taking his eyes off the ceiling.

"People . . . like you?"

"Yeah, not many kids at school know, but I was adopted," he said matter-of-factly.

"You . . . were?" Stephanie stammered.

"When I was real little. A baby. I don't remember my parents at all. Fortunately, things worked out well with the people who adopted me. My family, the Fletchers. But I've always wanted to find out who my real parents were. Just to meet them. Once."

"Gosh," said Stephanie, her breath coming out in a rush. "Wow. How long have you been looking?"

"I don't know. A couple of years."

"Oh," said Stephanie, her voice laced with disappointment. Two years! So much for her dream of spending the weekend with her mother. That was probably pretty unrealistic, anyway. But two years? And still no luck?

"Are you looking for someone, Stephanie?" asked Bruce. He was facing her now, his friendly eyes filled with concern.

Goose bumps rose on Stephanie's arms. She hesitated, torn by indecision. But finally she knew she had to tell Bruce. She wanted to find her mother, and Bruce could help. She stared into his honest hazel eyes for a long moment. She could trust Bruce. What she had to tell him would go no further than this room. She was sure of that.

"Yes," she said, almost inaudibly. "My . . . mother."

"We can help," said Bruce gently, filling her glass up. "I'm sure we can. Do you want to tell me about it?"

Tears filled Stephanie's eyes as a huge weight started to fall back from her shoulders. She wasn't expecting miracles, but at long last, she'd taken the first step. She'd found someone to share her pain. She sagged back into the chair.

Stephanie tried to concentrate on her chemistry notes, but her talk with Bruce that afternoon was still spinning around in her head. She'd felt drained after their session, but also excited. She'd love to tell Alex all about it, but . . .

She glanced over at her foster sister, who was lying on the den sofa, completely absorbed in her book. They were reading Hemingway in English class, and Alex was fascinated by his swashbuckling approach to life. She'd told Stephanie at least ten times in the past week of her plan to go to Pamplona for the annual running of the bulls, just as Papa had.

Stephanie couldn't understand, however, why anyone would want to risk his life trying to outrun stampeding bulls on the narrow streets of some tiny Spanish village. That was nuts. But then, many of the challenges Alex set for herself seemed kind of crazy. She admired her foster sister, though. Alex was tough. She was a real survivor, and that was something Stephanie understood only too well. She just didn't know if Alex would understand about *her* search for her mother.

In the end Stephanie decided not to tell her. She didn't want to give the Enomotos the impression she wasn't happy with them. Besides, Bruce had said it was very important not to get her hopes up. After all, he'd been looking for his parents for two years. Something might come through, and then again it might not.

The ringing of the phone came from far away, even though it was just next door in Dr. Enomoto's study.

"I'll get it," said Alex, jumping up and tearing out of the room.

Gazpacho dived under the nearest chair. Stephanie got down on her hands and knees to coax him out, keeping one ear open to the phone. Maybe it was Rick.

Alex's voice filtered through the walls. She sounded strangely upset. Soon the phone banged down, and Alex raced by and up the stairs. Stephanie heard her door slam. Gazpacho looked up with big, serious eyes.

"Maybe I'd better go find out what's wrong," Stephanie whispered in his fuzzy ear.

But upstairs, just as she was about to knock on Alex's door, Stephanie heard an incredible sound. Muffled sobs came from within. *Alex was crying!* Alex never cried. That was the amazing thing about her—she was always in control of her life. In fact, that's what had made Stephanie a little afraid of her.

Again she started for the door handle, then hesitated. She might embarrass Alex by barging in. Alex liked to handle her own problems. Stephanie thought of all the nights she'd cried herself to sleep and realized that, sure, she liked to handle her own problems, too, but sometimes it helped to know that someone cared. Like Bruce today.

Quietly Stephanie turned the handle and walked in.

"Alex?" she said softly, but Alex didn't respond. Her head was buried in her pillow, her body shaking with sobs. Stephanie sat down beside her and put a hand on Alex's arm.

"You want to talk about it?" she asked awkwardly. She'd never tried to comfort anyone before. Except Gazpacho. But cats didn't reject you. They were a safe bet. With Alex you didn't know.

"Uh . . . well, if there's anything I can do to help . . ." stammered Stephanie, patting Alex's arm.

"It's Wes," cried Alex.

"Is he . . . is he okay?" Stephanie asked.

"Yes . . . no . . . I don't know," said Alex, her sobs breaking out anew.

"Did he have an accident? He's not in the hospital, is he?"

"Yes . . ." said Alex, turning her reddened eyes on Stephanie.

"His car?"

"Yes," Alex said again. "He . . . he spun out on a curve at practice today. The car's totaled."

"Oh, no," exclaimed Stephanie. "Was that him on the phone?"

"Yes."

"Thank goodness. So he's okay?"

"Yeah, he's okay. He's got some scrapes and burns and stuff," said Alex bitterly. Then she sat up abruptly. "You should have heard him, Steph! You should have heard him telling me about it! Like the accident was some big joke! He was laughing! Actually laughing when he told me about hitting the wall and the flames and the car blowing up! It was sick! I couldn't believe it."

"Whew. That's what I call a pretty screwed-up sense of humor," said Stephanie, immediately forgetting her own awkwardness. "He could have been killed!"

Alex threw herself on her pillow again and burst into tears. "I know, Steph. That's what's destroying me. What if he dies next time? I couldn't take that again. Not after Noodle. I just couldn't take it."

Stephanie patted Alex's back. "Does he know how you feel?"

"Of course he does. But he tells me I don't understand, and I tell him he doesn't understand, so the discussion just kind of fizzles out each time."

"I guess you can't tell him not to race cars any more than he can tell you not to go off the ten-meter board, huh?"

"You're right," agreed Alex. "And that's what makes it so tough. I really care about Wes...a lot...and admire what he does, but I don't think I can stand the trauma of not knowing every time whether or not he's going to live through the next race. It was like that all through Noodle's last year. When I said good-bye to him in the morning, I never knew if I'd see him that night. One seizure could take him away." Alex turned her tear-stained face to

Stephanie. "Oh, Steph. It was terrible. I loved my brother so much. I wish you'd known him. He was so gentle and kind. And all through his sickness, he never complained. Never. Sometimes the pain was so bad, too. I could feel it. I used to pray to let my body take the pain away from him, if only for a little while, but there was nothing I could do. There was nothing anyone could do. We had to sit there and watch him die."

Stephanie watched Alex stare dejectedly at the floor, her mind obviously miles away, back with her dying brother. Back at the funeral. Back to the lonely house and Noodle's empty bedroom. Whew! For the first time Stephanie realized that Alex's life hadn't been so simple, either. Sure, she lived in a beautiful home with parents who loved her and had a great group of friends. Sure she was smart and a top-notch diver and would probably have some brilliant future. But none of this would bring back her brother. Nothing could ever fill the hole of his absence, ease the pain of his death. Alex had found the strength to go on by looking down into herself. In that way, she was like Stephanie, alone.

Stephanie stared at her sister, love and admiration welling up in her own heart. Alex was stronger than she'd ever imagined. She hadn't flipped out after Noodle's death or run away or rebelled against the unfairness of it. No, Alex had faced it all head on. Alex was a winner. But what she didn't need at this point in her life was to be involved with someone else living on the fringes of death. A person could only be so strong.

"Any chance Wes'll change?" asked Stephanie,

trying to sound hopeful.

Alex shook her head slowly. "His best friend, Harry, who raced for Firestone, died on the track about six months ago, but even that didn't slow him down."

"Then it seems to me, you're going to have to make a decision about whether or not you can handle staying with him . . . kind of like Rick and me." The words slipped out before Stephanie had a chance to stop herself.

"What do you mean?" said Alex, suddenly sitting up straight. "I thought things were going great with you two."

"They are . . . sort of," stammered Stephanie.

"What do you mean . . . sort of?" asked Alex.

Stephanie squirmed uncomfortably. It was one thing to help Alex with her problems, quite another to open up and share her own. But she saw only care and concern in Alex's brown eyes, and that gave her confidence.

"Well, I guess I don't have to tell you what different people Rick and I are," began Stephanie.

"That's okay. Look at Ginger and Craig. She's sophisticated New York and he's laid-back California, and you've got to admit that relationship's doing just fine."

Stephanie laughed. "Yeah, if I didn't know, I'd think they were Siamese twins."

"Attached at the mouth," Alex giggled.

Stephanie suddenly got serious. "But you know what I mean. They still come from the same kind of background. They can feel proud about what their parents do and compare the schools they've attended and the houses they've lived in. All I want to do is forget the crummy past. And that makes me feel really awkward and out of place with Rick sometimes. You know his father's even traced the Forrester family history back to England in the fifteenth century. How can I compete with that?"

"Steph," pleaded Alex. "You don't have to. You are who you are right now. Sure it must be great to have a fancy coat of arms to hang over the fireplace, but you don't like someone because of his coat of arms or his family's volumes of genealogy, do you? That doesn't make Rick any better than anyone else."

"You're right. I guess if I could just be honest with Rick about my past, things might be better."

"You mean even Rick doesn't know?" exclaimed Alex.

"Naw. I keep meaning to tell him, but the timing just hasn't been right. I don't know. I guess I'm really afraid he'll be disgusted and tell me to take a hike."

"Steph, give him a little more credit. Rick's one of the most sensitive people I know. I'm sure he'd understand."

"Yeah . . . maybe . . . I'll think about it." Stephanie stood up and ran her hands nervously down the sides of her jeans. Alex stood up beside her.

"Thanks a lot, Steph . . . for listening to me. I guess I needed it."

"Uh . . . no problem," Stephanie replied, some of the old awkwardness resurfacing. "Thanks for listening to me. I'll let you know when I get brave enough to talk to Rick. Don't hold your breath, though."

Alex laughed softly. "You nut!"

"It takes one to know one, huh?" Stephanie grinned at Alex, then ducked quickly out of the room.

Chapter Five

Stephanie was surprised to see a letter addressed to her, propped up on the kitchen table, when she got home from school the next day. She eyed it suspiciously. It was only the third letter she'd ever received in her life, and in the past, they'd usually spelled trouble. Like the time she was summoned to court on the shoplifting charge. But this envelope was thick and expensive looking, not some town official cheap paper. Stephanie picked it up and tore open the creamy envelope. Inside she found tissue and several different parts. As she read the contents, she began to feel sick.

"Alex! Alex!" she cried, running to the bottom of the stairs. The house was completely silent. Stephanie rushed from room to room and finally out the back door.

"Oh . . ." she said, hesitating on the doorstep. The whole gang was sitting around the picnic table munching cookies and sipping iced drinks.

"Come join us," called Lori, moving over on the bench.

"Naw . . . I can't," said Stephanie. "I . . . uh . . ."

"What is it, Steph?" asked Alex. "You look like you just saw a ghost. Everything okay?"

"Yeah . . . fine."

"Please, come have a glass of tea with us," pleaded Alex. Stephanie couldn't believe it. Alex was asking, not ordering for once. A lot of things had been different since their talk. She wandered over to the table and sat down.

"How'd your shopping trip go?" she asked, searching for something to say. She had been scheduled to hit the spring sales with them but had been forced to stay after school for a teacher's conference instead.

"Wonderful," said Elaine. "I got the most fabulous pair of pants."

"Yeah," broke in Alex, grinning broadly. "She looks kind of like a chic Charlie Chaplin."

"They're super baggy," Lori added.

"And they're neon blue!" said Kit. "Neon, shocking blue! Absolutely insane."

"That sounds neat," said Stephanie, shifting nervously in her seat. Why had she accepted their invitation? She had too much on her mind to listen to shopping tales.

"There's still a lot of great bargains on sale," Lori said. "If you want to go down and have a look sometime, I'd love to go with you."

"Yeah," said Stephanie. "I guess I could really use a new wardrobe. Any place sell really fancy stuff?"

"You mean fancy fancy like ball gowns?" asked Elaine.

"Uh . . . I don't know. I guess so," stammered Stephanie, concentrating on her glass of tea.

"Whew, you're talking some big bucks," Kit pointed out. "But the Emporium has a lot of gorgeous formal gowns on the second floor. You know the one that's carpeted, where everyone talks in whispers."

"Excuse me, Madam, but could I possibly be of assistance to you today?" said Alex, affecting the second-floor Emporium voice. "You're looking especially well, I might add. One of the outfits in our new line from France would be perfect for you. Beautiful ensembles start at a mere five hundred dollars. But because you are one of our esteemed customers, $499.95 for you."

Stephanie wished she could join in the laughter around her, but $500! Where was she going to get that kind of money?

"Is that what these things cost?" she asked, trying to keep the horror from her voice.

"Some of them," acknowledged Kit. "And some are even more expensive. Where are you planning to go? Surely not the old Glenwood High prom."

"Naw . . . " Stephanie said. "I was just wondering."

"Did you get your letter?" asked Alex. "Mom put it on the kitchen table."

"Yeah . . . " said Stephanie nervously. "Thanks. I . . . uh . . . gotta go."

"You mean you got a mysterious letter, from the outside world, and you're not going to share it with us?" Elaine asked in mock horror. "What have we done to deserve such treatment?"

"Aw . . . it was nothing . . . really."

"Well, it sure looked impressive," said Alex. "I bet it took two trees just to make the envelope."

Even Stephanie had to giggle.

"Well, if you really want to know," she said, "it was an invitation."

"To the Presidential Ball in Washington, I presume?" said Kit.

"No, I went last year and it was really too, too boring," joked Stephanie, her cheeks turning pink when everyone laughed. "Actually it was an invitation to Rick's sister's wedding."

"Why waste your time with the Presidential Ball when you can go to a really formal event, huh?" quipped Alex. "When is it?"

"This Saturday," Stephanie replied.

"Whew, that's going to be some fancy occasion, I bet," Kit broke in.

"You wouldn't believe it," said Stephanie, her words coming out in a rush. For the next ten minutes she filled them in on all the details. She even showed them the personal note from Mrs. Forrester apologizing for sending out an invitation at the last minute—the rest had been mailed several weeks ago, long before she'd met Stephanie. Now that she'd had that pleasure, she said she hoped Stephanie would honor them with her presence on Saturday.

"Wow!" cried Alex. "How exciting!"

"Oh, Steph, you're going to have such a lovely time," said Lori. "It'll be beautiful, I'm sure."

"What are you going to wear?" Kit asked.

"I...I don't know," moaned Stephanie, dropping her head in her hands. "That's what's giving me the creeps about this whole thing. Everyone's going to look really chi-chi. What am I going to do?"

"You're going to go and look absolutely stunning and have a wonderful time," said Alex, sitting up straight on the bench.

"You don't think they'll eat me alive?" asked Stephanie in a small voice.

"Hey, you have as much right to be there as anyone, so don't sweat it, kid," Kit said. "We've got faith in you. You can handle anything. Go and have fun—for us."

Stephanie shrugged her shoulders. "Yeah, sure... well, see you around." She swaggered off, her knees still weak with fear. Of course they thought she could handle anything. Isn't that what she'd been telling them ever since she arrived in Glenwood? Well now she'd just have to prove it.

"I don't know, Alex," Stephanie said, staring at the pale lavender formal lying on the bed. "It seems awfully dressy."

"I wore it to the prom last year. It's not that posh. Besides, you said this was going to be fancy, didn't you?" Alex pulled another dress from her closet. "What about this?"

Rick was picking her up for the wedding in two hours, and Stephanie still hadn't decided what to wear. Maybe it was kind of dumb to leave it until the last minute like this, but Alex had assured her that she had plenty of dresses for Stephanie to choose from. Besides, Stephanie had been subconsciously trying not to think about the big society wedding. She wanted to be there with Rick, but she would have preferred to attend as a fly on the wall. If only she could simply observe, and not be called upon to speak!

"No, green definitely is not my color," she said, shaking her head. "With my pale complexion, it makes me look like a piece of seaweed."

Alex laughed. "Okay, the green cocktail dress is definitely out. So we're down to the lavender or the cream."

The girls stared at the clothes.

"You sure you won't let me call the others in on this?" said Alex finally. "They're so much better at fashion than I am. You know me, I'd probably show up in my favorite overalls, the ones I fix the car in."

Stephanie laughed. "No, you and I can decide. It can't be that big a deal." She definitely didn't want to involve the others; everyone picking over her, telling her how to fix her hair, how to put on makeup. She knew they'd be kind and helpful, but she didn't want to be the center of that kind of attention. "Why don't I go with the lavender? The cream looks too much like a wedding dress, I think."

"Okay, you go have a shower and I'll iron this thing," ordered Alex.

For the next couple of hours the two girls worked frantically to get Stephanie ready. Alex brushed her hair until it glowed. They redid her makeup three times—Stephanie had to wash her face and completely start over each time—but finally she looked just right. Best of all, the lavender gown fit perfectly. It was strapless so it showed off Stephanie's slender, pale shoulders to perfection; and the tight bodice and full, flowing skirt made her fine figure look ravishing. Elaine had lent her two silver combs which held her hair back elegantly from her face. The rest tumbled down her bare back.

"You look great!" announced Alex when they'd finished. "Wow! I wish Mom and Dad were here to see you. What a weekend to be locked away in some convention with a bunch of zit specialists."

Stephanie laughed and whirled around giddily in front of the mirror. Even she couldn't believe the transformation. She looked . . . beautiful. Impulsively she threw her arms around Alex.

"Thanks, Alex. Thanks a lot."

The doorbell rang. The two girls locked eyes, then Alex raced downstairs. Stephanie stood there a moment, trying to get herself calmed down, then followed slowly. Pausing at the top of the stairs, she watched Rick enter. He looked so stunning in his black tux, so handsome and mature that it took her breath away. His usually unruly curls were under control, but his grin was still kind of crooked and . . . Rickish. When he looked up and saw her, Stephanie felt her face grow warm. For a moment he didn't say anything, and she began to tremble.

"Stephanie!" he said softly, almost as if he were in awe of her. "You look amazing. Absolutely amazing."

After that, Stephanie floated down the stairs, barely feeling her feet touch the steps. Immediately Rick took her hands in his and kissed her on the cheek.

"Won't I be the envy of every male at the party?"

His eyes glowed warmly down at her. Alex gave her the thumbs-up sign behind Rick's back.

"Uh . . . thanks," replied Stephanie. She enjoyed the attention, but was so unused to it that it made her feel a little uneasy.

"I'm sorry the wedding invitation came so late," said Rick on the ride over to his house. "But as Mom explained in her note, she sent the others out ages ago. I had to scrounge around to find that one. Probably the one meant for the big scrapbook Mom's planning to do of this wedding."

Stephanie laughed. "You mean those big fat albums that have everything but a piece of the cake glued in?"

"You got it, although knowing Mom she'll figure out some way to fit the cake in, too."

Stephanie smiled and relaxed a bit. Knowing Rick had sent her the invitation specially, that she hadn't been just another name on a long list of distant social acquaintances, made her feel very special. Not to mention his mother's sweet note. At least they seemed to really want her there.

Anyway, she mused, how long could it all last? In another couple of hours or so, she would be back in her jeans and maybe she and Rick would be lying on the beach somewhere watching the sun set. She shivered with pleasure at the thought.

By the time they turned into the drive, Stephanie felt that things were under control. She felt silly to have even freaked out in the first place.

The minute Rick opened her car door she could hear the chatter and laughter of the other guests, and her knees felt weak again. They were probably all old friends with plenty to say to each other. Well, at least she had Rick. Struggling out of the low car, she forgot about her long dress and tripped over the skirt. As she walked, the heels of Alex's shoes kept sinking in the cracks between the cobblestones, forcing her to cling to Rick. All at once, Stephanie felt clumsy and awkward.

But when they entered the courtyard by the pool, she momentarily forgot her fears. Shimmering in the noonday sun, a land of make-believe was laid out before her. Water lilies floated in the pool, suffusing the air with a heavenly fragrance, and urns of all-white flowers stood against the white adobe walls. In the middle of everything rose up an arch of flowers. Rick explained that the bride and groom would walk through it to get married and gestured to the rows and rows of white chairs facing in that direction. The ten-piece orchestra was already in place on a raised platform. They were playing the kind of music Stephanie had always hated, but here, right now, it seemed perfect.

"I've got to leave you now," said Rick, squeezing her hand.

Stephanie looked up at him, suddenly terror stricken. "What . . . what do you mean . . . leave?"

"My sister wants me to be part of the action, so I have to go play usher. I'll catch up with you after the ceremony." He kissed her cheek and was gone.

Stephanie's heart sank as she watched him walk through the crowd, smiling at people, stopping to greet others. It was all so natural to him, the whole formal scene. It would never occur to him that she was scared stiff. As she watched, Marcia Connors materialized out of the throng and slipped her arm around Rick's waist. He kissed her cheek. Stephanie's face burned. They made a stunning couple, Stephanie realized, so tall and tanned . . . and perfect. But why was Marcia here at all?

All at once Stephanie realized something else. She looked around with horror and saw that she was the only person at the wedding in a long dress. All the other women had on short cocktail dresses that smacked of designer labels and big bucks. Marcia's dress was a straight sheath of rose-colored satin that shimmered in the sunlight. It looked cool and elegant, and at her neck and wrist she wore simple, but heavy gold jewelry. Stephanie thought of her own bare neck and the plain silver chain around her wrist.

Tears stung her eyes, but she blinked them back, determined not to let a bunch of rich jerks intimidate her. Yet she couldn't stop staring at some of the ladies. One had on a dress that was a mass of pale green ruffles all over. Her tanned arms and legs stuck out of it like the delicate stalks of an exotic flower. Another had on a 1920s style dress covered in tiny red beads that sparkled radiantly. Alex would like that one, mused Stephanie, since it's more of a costume than a dress. Her eye wandered from dress to dress, overwhelmed by the designs, the expensive fabrics, and the magnificent jewelry. Colors of every hue in the rainbow paraded around the courtyard. But no one had on anything that looked even close to her dress. She'd made a big mistake not getting the rest of the gang in on her outfit. Lori would have known exactly what to wear.

"Why hello, Stephanie," cooed Marcia, sliding up to her. "I like your dress. Are you a bridesmaid or something?"

"No," replied Stephanie stiffly. "It's Alex's."

"Oh, I thought I recognized it. Didn't she wear it to the prom last year?" Stephanie cringed.

"I wasn't here last year. What do I know?"

"Of course not. Anyway, it really is beautiful." She flashed Stephanie a smile, then pulled away. "Well, I've got to go help Isabelle and Richard. I'm sure they're wondering where I am. Isn't this all so exciting?"

"If you like Disneyland," Stephanie shot back.

Marcia didn't seem to know what to say to that. Giving Stephanie a strange look, she wandered off.

"Bride or groom," came a deep voice close to her ear. Stephanie jumped. A tall, slender man dressed just like Rick held his arm out for her. Stephanie stared at him in confusion. What did he mean bride or groom? She was obviously not either.

"Are you a member of the bride's party or the groom's?" the man continued patiently, putting Stephanie's hand on his arm.

"Oh . . . yes . . . of course," stuttered Stephanie, her face coloring. "The bride's."

It took all her courage to hold her head high as she was led down the aisle and into a seat near the front. Let them stare, she thought haughtily. There's no way I'm going to give them the pleasure of seeing my knees knock.

Stephanie soon forgot the people around her as she watched Rick lead various ladies to their seats. Her heart melted at his elegant assurance, but occasionally he'd glance over at her and make a silly face. It was so quick probably no one else saw it, but Stephanie was delighted and had to bite her tongue to keep from laughing out loud.

Finally, with a dramatic flourish, the orchestra started to play the processional. The ceremony had begun. When Stephanie turned and saw Isabelle poised at the end of the aisle, toward the back of the courtyard, she felt goose bumps rise on her arms. Isabelle looked like a fairy princess. Her waves of golden hair were sprinkled with baby's breath and her long white dress seemed to glow with its own joyous light. Somehow Stephanie had imagined an electronics design engineer would look kind of the way Elaine used to, with thick glasses and frumpy clothes. Stephanie sighed. To be so beautiful and smart—some girls really had it all.

The ceremony was short but very special. It was the first wedding Stephanie had ever been to, and it seemed incredibly romantic. The bride and groom had written it themselves, and there wasn't a dry eye left when the minister finally pronounced them married.

Marcia was the first to throw her arms around Isabelle in congratulations. This broke the magic spell for Stephanie, and she hurried through a side gate to escape the crowds. She didn't want Isabelle to see that her brother had picked the girl with the worst taste to accompany him to the wedding. She found a bench buried deep in a rose garden and slumped down. A few minutes later, she heard laughter and the clink of champagne glasses as other guests approached.

"Can you imagine showing up for a noon wedding in a formal?" came one woman's voice through the tangle of vines a few minutes later.

"Maybe she thought she was so beautiful, she could set the style."

Stephanie felt so angry, she was dizzy.

"Like Princess Diana." The sound of their cruel laughter ripped through Stephanie's soul.

"Oh, well, maybe she's the gardener's daughter or something and had to be invited. It's so important to keep the servants happy."

"Do I ever know what you mean. My chauffeur . . ."

Their voices trailed off as they passed out of earshot. Stephanie felt as if she were coming down with a deadly fever. Her skin burned, and her blood pounded madly inside her head. Her hands were shaking so badly, she had to sit on them.

Okay, she thought bitterly, so I don't look like all those jerks. Maybe I don't want to look like them, either. I'd rather take the money they spend on their stupid wardrobes and do some good in the world. There's probably enough bucks around this place to end world hunger. What a bunch of selfish jerks.

"There you are."

Stephanie jumped at the sound of Rick's voice. Her first instinct was to run into the safety of his arms, feel his secure warmth, and forget about the nightmare around her, but she held back. After all, this *was* Rick's world—most likely he thought she looked ridiculous, too. Rick smiled and offered her his hand.

"I've been looking all over the place for you. What happened? Is everything okay?"

"I just got claustrophobic," Stephanie said defensively. "All those people . . ."

"Yeah, I know what you mean. Mother's crew is a little hard to take all at once. But wasn't the ceremony great—I mean, like a movie or something?"

"It was okay," Stephanie snapped. "I've seen better."

"Oh," said Rick, looking like he'd just been slapped.

"Well, I hope you get a chance to talk with my sister before she leaves today," he continued patiently.

"Maybe. But I imagine there are a few other people on her list before me." Stephanie fought to keep the sarcasm out of her voice, but lost.

"Actually, she told me this morning she was looking forward to meeting you. I think you two would have a lot in common."

Stephanie almost laughed out loud. She and Isabelle could talk solidly for a week and a half and never find a single thread in their lives that was similar. They were worlds apart. Couldn't Rick see that?

"Yeah . . . we both wore long dresses to the wedding," Stephanie shot back.

"Hey, what's happening?" said Rick suddenly, dropping her arm.

"What do you mean?" Stephanie said, her heart pounding. She wasn't in the mood to explain anything. All she wanted to do was get out of there, put some serious mileage between herself and these stupid people.

"I mean, you're acting like I've superoffended you or something. At least tell me what I've done before you come down on me like this."

"Like what?" snapped Stephanie.

"Like every time I say anything, you bite my head off. What gives?"

Stephanie squirmed uncomfortably. "I guess this circus just isn't my scene," she mumbled, staring at the ground.

"This 'circus' happens to be my sister's wedding," said Rick hotly.

"Good for her! May she live happily ever after," cried Stephanie, desperately.

"I'm sure she will. Too bad I can't say the same for you. I don't know what chip you're carrying around on your shoulder, Stephanie, but you'd better figure out some way to knock it off before you ruin your life totally."

"Hey, Forrester, why don't you let me worry about my life, and you worry about yours, okay?" Stephanie started to stomp off, but when he didn't reply, she hesitated and glanced back. Rick was staring after her with a mixture of hurt and anger.

"Because I care about you, Stephanie," he said quietly. "At least I thought I did."

"Well, don't!" she snapped. "I'm not worth it. Go back to your rich friends. Go find Marcia. I'm sure she's lost without you."

"Come on, Steph," said Rick, taking a step toward her. "Let's not destroy what we've got. Talk to me. What's wrong?"

"Like I told you," Stephanie said, her voice trembling as she turned her back on him. She knew she'd weaken if she stared into Rick's eyes for one second longer, and there was no way she was going back to that wedding. No way. "This just isn't my scene, man. I've never seen a bigger bunch of fakes in all my life."

Rick grabbed her shoulder and spun her around. His eyes were flashing fire. For a moment Stephanie was frightened. "I gues your idea of a 'real person' is Kirk Wallace, huh?" he demanded.

"Ouch," wailed Stephanie wiggling to get free. "Get your hands off me. You're hurting me."

"Well, what do you think you've just done to me?" he said, increasing his grip. "Admit it. You'd rather be with Kirk Wallace and his bunch of vultures than here. Isn't that what you're trying to tell me?"

"Yeah... yeah. That's it," cried Stephanie, feeling like a cornered rat. "At least they don't have their heads so far up their..."

"Shut up, Stephanie!" demanded Rick. "Before you make a bigger fool out of yourself than you already have."

Stephanie stared at him a second, her eyes blazing. Then, without another word, she turned and ran. Hastily, she made her way around the back side of the house to avoid the wedding reception which was going on full blast. Part of her wanted to cry, while another part was glad she and Rick had just broken up. A strange sense of relief filtered through her anger.

The noise of the party faded as she made her way farther and farther down the drive. Her only thought was to escape. She didn't want to think about anything right now. She wanted to get home, to the safety of her room before she tried to sort things out, before she gave in to the tears that were now dangerously close to the surface. But how was she going to get herself back to town? Stephanie hesitated, unsure of herself for the millionth time that day. Well, she finally decided, she'd just have to stick out her thumb. It had always gotten her where she wanted before.

Chapter Six

Stephanie giggled. If she thought she looked ridiculous before, she must really look outrageous now. She was reminded of a scene in *Smokey and the Bandit* when Sally Field was standing beside the road in her wedding gown thumbing a ride. Now, if Burt Reynolds would only come by and pick me up, too, she thought.

A gentle breeze sprang up, tossing her hair about her delicate face. Holding her shoes in her hand, Stephanie strode on, barefoot, filling her lungs with the clean, fresh air. Freedom, she thought, how sweet it is!

She paused at an overlook to take in the view below: the endless fields with the wide, slow river snaking through them. The hills in the distance. The sea beyond, lost somewhere in the haze. The clear blue sky overhead. This is where she belonged—not with people, but out here, on her own, as part of the landscape, part of the universe.

But Stephanie couldn't deny the pain in her heart. Things were over with Rick. He'd never want to see her again after this. But actually, she'd done him a favor. He could relax and enjoy the party now. He wouldn't have to explain who his weird date was—the one wearing the old-fashioned formal. Maybe he was thankful she'd gone.

Picking up her pace, Stephanie walked through the shadows of the old eucalyptus trees, down the last twist of the drive and past the final stand of fancy cars. She didn't even look at them. Right now, they neither impressed nor scared her.

When she reached the main road, she considered walking all the way to Glenwood. It was such a beautiful day and her body was charged with energy. But it was five miles, and she was barefoot—Alex's heels had been killing her. She'd never make it. Stephanie stuck out her thumb.

The first car shot past her: some guy and his girl friend oblivious of everything except each other. The next car slowed up, and the whole family, complete with two dogs and a cat, stared at her, but moved on without stopping.

She heard the next car long before it arrived. She recognized the low, ominous rumbling sound that told of a powerful engine. It was approaching fast, and when it swung around the corner, Stephanie wanted to leap into the ditch and hide. *Kirk Wallace!* But he'd already seen her.

"Well, hello, babe. You practicing for homecoming queen or something?" he called out after gliding to a halt before her.

"Naw . . . just wandering around looking at the view. Too bad you're spoiling it." She hoped she sounded tough. Maybe he'd give up and just leave.

"Yeah, it is beautiful, isn't it?"

Stephanie glanced at him quickly. What was this switch? He actually sounded like a normal person.

"Yeah, sure," she stammered. "Well, I guess I better be getting back to the wedding. People are going to start wondering what happened to me."

"You do that," said Kirk. "Hey . . . and give my regards to all the beautiful people, will ya?"

As Stephanie started to back away from the car, she heard voices approaching. Her heart pounded. Were the guests leaving already? The voices got closer.

"Uh . . . Kirk, could I bum a ride back to town?" she asked. "I was leaving the party anyway. Things are winding up. I don't want to hassle Rick right now. He's got to say good-bye to people and stuff."

"Sure, kid, hop in."

Stephanie slid in quickly, and Kirk peeled out just as the group of people started unlocking a shiny black Mercedes.

"Well, kid, you don't exactly look like you had the time of your life. What happened? Did the dazzle of diamonds wear you out, or what?" Kirk asked. Stephanie cringed at his sarcasm, but was glad to see that, at least, he hadn't been drinking.

"I don't want to talk about it, Kirk," she said wearily.

"That bad, huh?"

"Worse."

"Hmmm, well you sure do look nice, though. I bet you were a hit?" Stephanie looked at him sharply, and was amazed to see that he wasn't being sarcastic. Instead, his face was kind and concerned. Yet another side of the enigmatic Kirk Wallace. She wondered how long it would take to really get a handle on where he was coming from. He could be so nice and then so horrible.

"Thanks," said Stephanie, relaxing a little back against the seat. "But I don't think anyone in that crowd appreciated my outfit."

"Screw 'em," growled Kirk. "Who needs 'em anyway, right?"

"Amen," Stephanie agreed. She rolled down the window and let the air wash over her. It really was a beautiful day. Now, out here with Kirk, she could finally enjoy it.

"What were you doing up here today?" asked Stephanie, lulled into a more peaceful mood by the motion of the car and the sweet smells of spring.

"Aw...just driving around...sort of," hedged Kirk.

"All by yourself?" That didn't sound like Kirk. He usually didn't move without his group of friends.

"Yeah, me and the old man had another blowup. I had to get away and cool off."

Stephanie noticed the dark circles under Kirk's eyes. He really looked worn out.

"You guys fight a lot?" asked Stephanie.

Kirk gave a short, harsh laugh. "Let's just say we've never been good friends, but he usually doesn't mess with me anymore... not since I knocked his block off two years ago."

"You hit your father! Why?"

"What do you want me to do, stand there and let him knock my brains out first? No more. Not for this kid. The old man wants to play rough with me, he's going to have to pay for it."

"Wow, I had some trouble like that in foster homes, but I didn't think that happened when you had real parents."

"I don't really think he means to—he just gets liquored up and goes kind of crazy."

"What does your mom say about all this?" Stephanie asked.

"My mom's... dead," said Kirk quietly.

"Geez, I'm sorry," Stephanie said. "Real sorry."

"Yeah, she died when I was thirteen. One neat lady, I tell you. She deserved a better life than the one she had with my dad, too. I always dreamed of giving it to her, but..."

Sudden tears filled Kirk's eyes.

They rode along in silence for a while, the car winding slowly over the hills and through the valleys. The sun went under a cloud, and the air grew cooler. Summer was still a long way away.

"Foster homes, huh? So what happened to your parents?" asked Kirk finally.

"I'm not sure," Stephanie told him. "I must have had a father, I guess, but I don't know anything about him. I remember my mother... sort of. She had a wonderful voice and I think she was very pretty. At least that's how I remember her. Maybe I've just made it up 'cause I want a pretty mother."

"Where is she now?"

"I don't know." Stephanie twisted her fingers in her lap. "She gave me up to foster care when I was five."

"And you've never heard from her since?" asked Kirk, horrified. "She gave you away... just like that?"

"Yeah, but maybe she had a reason," said Stephanie defensively. "Maybe she was really poor and wanted a better life for me. Maybe it was really hard for her to give me up. I don't know, but that's what I'm going to believe. That's what I've got to believe."

"Sure," said Kirk sympathetically. "I can see that. I always try to believe my mother is happier now that she's free of my dad. I need to believe that, too. Keeps me from going crazy."

"So why don't you leave your father?" asked Stephanie. "I mean, if he's so bad to you."

Kirk was silent for a moment, then said with a short laugh, "It's funny. I've thought about it, but I never could bring myself to actually walk out. He's my dad. He's all I've got in the world. And I guess he has his problems too and needs understanding. I just don't think I reach him. That's what drives me nuts."

"I wonder if rich people have all these problems." Stephanie sighed. "They always seem to be laughing and having a good time."

"Well, why shouldn't they?" snorted Kirk. "They're rich, aren't they?"

"Yeah... maybe. I just wonder sometimes. That's all." Stephanie stared out the window. Did Rick have problems with his parents? She couldn't imagine it.

They seemed so warm and close. But...

"So how was it being a foster kid?" asked Kirk. "Pretty tough, huh?"

"I didn't think so at first," Stephanie replied, thoughtfully. "You can get used to any kind of life if you have to...and I had to. But it got a bit rough when I got older. One of my foster fathers put the big move on me once. I didn't even understand what was going on...I just thought he was being nice...until he started putting his hands all over me. Really flipped me out."

Kirk crashed his fist down on the steering wheel. "What a miserable jerk! Did you report him?"

"Naw...I was too scared. Nothing happened anyway, because my foster mother came in and broke it up."

"Boy, would I ever love to get my hands on him," said Kirk angrily. "He'd be mincemeat when I finished. Mincemeat!"

Stephanie couldn't believe that this was the same Kirk who'd strutted around Stillwell Beach that day refusing to take her home. Now he wanted to protect her! It was kind of nice. Sometimes she got tired of always looking after herself. In some ways Kirk understood things about her no one else ever would. They hadn't been through it. Kirk had.

"Turn up this road, Kirk," said Stephanie suddenly.

"Huh...what?"

"I've been here once. There's a great view from the top."

They wound slowly up the hill, hugging the road on hairpin turns. At the top was a pull-off that Stephanie directed him into. She hopped out of the car, pulling him after her.

"Look. Isn't that beautiful?" She sighed, staring out over the valley that dropped away to the sea. The late-afternoon sun was just above the water, a giant orange ball suspended in the crystal-clear air. Stephanie breathed deeply and turned to look at Kirk.

"Yeah, I guess so," said Kirk, looking kind of bewildered.

"I love watching the sunset," Stephanie continued. "It's like there's something going on in the world that's bigger than all of us. Always makes my problems seem kind of small. Know what I mean?"

"Uh . . . not really," replied Kirk. "I just like the colors."

"Oh, me too. But can't you see that the sun setting is sort of like religion?" cried Stephanie, trying to make him understand. "It's been going down and coming up for millions of years, but there's no guarantee it'll be there tomorrow. You just have to have faith." She paused, drinking in the beauty of the wind. "Think of all the things the sun has seen: the dinosaurs, Columbus reaching the new world, the first train. Don't you find that overwhelming?"

"Yeah . . . when you put it like that," Kirk said, but Stephanie could tell he wasn't into it at all. Rick would have understood. Rick would have appreciated it the same way she did. In a flash Stephanie realized that even though she and Kirk had gotten close with their talk that afternoon, she still needed something more from a partner. She needed Rick. But there was no more Rick. Not after today. A sharp pain wrenched her heart, and a feeling of despair filled her. Stephanie stared, unseeingly, across the horizon as the realization of all that she had lost hit her.

"I guess I'd better get on home," said Stephanie, her voice echoing in the quiet.

"Me, too. Maybe my dad's sober by now."

"I'm really sorry about all that, Kirk . . . all you have to put up with. But my life got better, maybe yours will, too."

"Maybe . . ." he said and got into the car. "Maybe."

They rode the thirty or so miles back to Glenwood in silence, but it was a comfortable silence.

When they pulled up in front of the Enomotos', Stephanie felt a little embarrassed that her foster parents might see her with Kirk and his hot-rod car and disapprove, but she scolded herself silently. Kirk was her friend. The afternoon had sealed that. People were just going to have to understand that.

"Steph, I've really enjoyed today," said Kirk.

"Me, too. Thanks for rescuing me." Stephanie smiled warmly over at him.

"Well, you really helped me out when you took my knife the other day. I appreciated that."

"Okay, but don't ever use it in that way again, okay?" Stephanie cautioned him.

Kirk moved over in the seat and rested his arm behind her. Stephanie shrank against the door.

"Hey, it was no problem, but maybe you should come get it sometime. If I get caught with that thing, it'll be all over. Old Morrison's just looking for some excuse to get me suspended. I think I skipped class one too many times when I first got here."

"He's got your number, huh?" Kirk's arm had slipped down onto her shoulders.

"And then some," said Stephanie, laughing nervously. "Well, thanks a lot for everything, Kirk. See you around."

"Hey, hey. Not so fast. How about we take in a movie or something tonight?"

"Uh . . ."

"You can't be going out with that rich kid after running away from his sister's wedding today."

"No, I'm not, but I'm exhausted," she said, hating to be reminded how much Rick didn't want to see her. "It's been a long day."

"Ah, Steph, come on. We had such a good time today. Things are going great. Let's not stop it now. I really dig you."

"I like you too, Kirk . . . as a friend. So let's not ruin that, okay? I really have to go."

Kirk pulled angrily away. "I bet if I had a fat bank account and a hot Ferrari, you wouldn't say no. You know, you're just like those people you ran away from today, Stephanie. A fake. A complete fake. Well great, you go on in. You sit in your big, expensive house that doesn't even belong to you and you have a wonderful time. 'Cause I'm going out and have one fine time. Now get out."

He kicked open her door and pushed her through.

"Come on, Kirk. Don't ruin a good friendship. Don't act like this," pleaded Stephanie. She knew where he was coming from—he had been rejected, and he was hurt. In the world they both had been brought up in, when someone hurt you, you lashed back . . . with everything you had. That's what survival was all about.

"Friendship! Ha! What do you know? Get out of my way, Burroughs."

The door slammed shut as he stepped on the accelerator and spun away from the Enomotos' with a frightening squeal of tires. Slowly, Stephanie walked toward the house; by the time she got to the door, her face was wet with tears.

Chapter Seven

"So, how was it?" asked Elaine, dropping her tray down on the table beside Stephanie.

"Yeah, we want all the details . . . from beginning to end," chimed in Kit, peeling the top off her yogurt container.

"It must have been amazing," Lori said. "Absolutely amazing. I read the write-up in Sunday's paper."

Stephanie concentrated on her lunch. She wished Alex was here to help her out, but she was at the pool getting in some extra practice for the big meet Friday. Stephanie had given Alex a brief rundown of the wedding while they were on their way to the races yesterday. Stephanie didn't really like car racing but she didn't want to be home if Rick called. She didn't feel strong enough for a confrontation. She still hadn't sorted everything out in her own head yet; she kept going back and forth between anger at Rick, and his type, and the realization that her own insecurities had freed her to judge him too harshly. Had she lost him for good, though? Stephanie was almost afraid to find out.

"I bet there were a lot of beautiful people," sighed Lori.

"Yeah . . . there were," replied Stephanie.

"Well . . . ?" urged Kit.

"Well what?" Stephanie snapped.

"That's all you're going to tell us! The wedding of the century hits sleepy old Glenwood and that's all you've got to say about it! Steph, we're dying! Tell us all!"

"You read the papers. It was just like they said," said Stephanie, trying to sound bored with the whole subject. "It was a pull-all-the-stops-out affair. Isn't that what the *San Francisco Chronicle* called it?"

"You mean it was in the San Francisco papers, too?" exclaimed Lori. "I just read the *Palo Alto Times*. Wow, it must have really been something!"

"Yeah, it was if you enjoy watching a bunch of jerks trying to prove how rich and successful they all are. I found it pretty disgusting."

"Wasn't it a little bit fun to pretend you were one of them?" Kit sighed. "Just for an afternoon? Alex said you looked the part—absolutely gorgeous."

"I wish we'd seen you," Lori said. "I bet you looked great."

"Yeah, kind of like a clown in a circus," choked Stephanie bitterly. Abruptly, she got up from the table and made her way through the crowded lunch-room to the exit. She knew they were trying to be nice, but the pain she felt was too raw. She wanted to forget all about Saturday.

"Steph! Please... wait up!" Stephanie froze, her heart hammering at the sound of the familiar voice. She turned as Rick caught up with her in the hallway. His warm brown eyes burned into her, and the white of his shirt blurred before her eyes as tears threatened. If she could only lay her head on his chest and forget everything else. She needed him so much. "Steph, I think we should talk."

"I can't now," said Stephanie gruffly. "I've got an appointment with my counselor. Gotta go."

"Steph, please, there's been a terrible misunderstanding. I've got to talk to you. We've got to straighten things out."

You mean, you've got to tell me to take a hike, thought Stephanie bitterly. Kirk had been right: getting mixed up with Rick Forrester was making her miserable. Very, very miserable. But whatever Rick had to say, she ought to go ahead and hear it. He certainly deserved that.

"Okay," she began. "What..."

"Richard, there you are!" Stephanie turned to see Marcia Connors bearing down on them, looking perfectly groomed and fresh. Her face was radiant.

"Oh... hello, Stephanie," she said acknowledging Stephanie's presence with a quick nod of her head before linking her arm through Rick's.

"Marcia, just a minute..." he began.

"Oh Richard, I had the most wonderful time with you and your family on Saturday. You were really too good to me." She flashed him a generous smile.

"Marcia, Stephanie and I . . ." Again he was cut off.

"Oh, but you must help me." She pouted. "I have racked my brain till I've grown quite desperate trying to think of the perfect present for Isabelle. It's got to be perfectly right for her. Help me."

"I . . ." stammered Rick.

"Well . . . I mean . . . what's her crystal pattern? Or silver? Tiffany's has the most divine pair of candlesticks. I presume she's registered at Tiffany's, isn't she?"

Stephanie shook her head and marched off. Marcia had brought back all of Saturday's nightmare, plus some. Stephanie hadn't even thought of getting Isabelle a gift. Rick was probably horrified by this failing, too.

As she started up the stairs to her class on the second floor, a poster caught Stephanie's attention. It advertised the tennis clinic offered to beginners each Monday. Stephanie stared at the poster for a moment, then moved on. Taking tennis lessons was like admitting she wanted to be part of Rick's crowd. Well, forget it.

But she couldn't. The poster haunted her all day. It had been thrilling to hit that tennis ball squarely and watch it sail neatly over the net. Secretly she'd always wanted to try a sport, but the thought of failing always held her back. Well, if the class that afternoon was for beginners, what did she have to lose? She wasn't doing this for Rick, she was doing it for herself.

At three-fifteen, Stephanie was dressed in her PE outfit with Gayle Rogers's racket in her hand. She hated the PE outfit; it always made her look super-skinny, but it would have to do. She peered out of the locker room cautiously, then slipped into the empty hall. A wolf whistle instantly split the air.

"Let's see," said Kirk Wallace, sauntering up. "On Saturday we were homecoming queen. Now we're Chrissy Evert. You're really coming up in the world, kid. What'll it be tomorrow? Princess Diana?"

"Aw, Kirk, give me a break," retorted Stephanie, her cheeks burning.

"Kid, I've given you more breaks than you'll ever know—many more than you deserve. That's why you should be a little nicer to me, 'cause I can make things rough for you. Really rough." His laugh sent shudders down Stephanie's spine.

Quickly, she tried to edge past him, but he blocked her way.

"Hey, I just want to talk to you, kid. What's wrong with that? You sure didn't run away when you needed me on Saturday, now, did you?"

"I had a nice time with you Saturday, Kirk," Stephanie said. "But I'm late for my tennis lesson. Please . . . let me go."

"How about giving me my knife back first? I feel real lost without it."

"Okay. Sure. Fine. I'll get it." Stomping off to her locker, Stephanie spun the lock angrily. She wanted this over—fast. But when she reached up for the knife, everything on the top shelf came down. Books and papers tumbled out, and the knife slid across the hall . . . bouncing off Rick's shoe as he passed by. Stephanie gasped.

"Now who does this go back to?" said Rick, picking up the knife. His face was hard and expressionless. "Stephanie? Kirk?"

Stephanie could feel the blood drain from her face; she tried to speak, but the words caught in her throat. How could she ever explain?

"Hey, man, that's my hardware," snarled Kirk. "Hand it over."

"With pleasure," said Rick icily, formally presenting the handle of the knife to Kirk, who took it and fled. Without even glancing at Stephanie, Rick continued walking down the hall.

There were six other students in the beginning tennis class, all of them from lower classes. They met at the old tennis courts as the varsity and junior varsity teams practiced on the new, spiffy ones. They didn't even get a real tennis coach, just the boys' PE teacher, who also happened to be a decent tennis player. But no one seemed to mind, and once they got playing, Stephanie shed her inhibitions completely. She didn't care that she was the only senior in the bunch—it felt great to pound out her frustrations on the court. And Mr. Emerson's compliments kept her working harder and harder.

"Burroughs, I think you've got some talent," he said at the end of practice. "You're good."

Stephanie smiled up at him and pushed a damp strand of hair out of her face. She was hot and tired, but the compliment charged her with energy.

"Yep, I think we might make a tennis player out of you. Do you want to go for it?"

Stephanie nodded eagerly. "Sure. I'd love to."

"Well look, if you agree to work your buns off, I'll

give you a lesson every day, and maybe . . . just maybe we can get you in the intramurals this year. What do you say?"

"Wow! The intramurals! In three weeks!" The intramural competition was only among the students at Glenwood, usually kids who weren't good enough to be on a varsity team, but at least she might get a chance to prove herself to her school.

"I think we can do it. You like a challenge, don't you?" Mr. Emerson teased, grinning. Usually teachers always gave her a rough time. This was a switch.

"Sure."

"Then we're going for it. Be out here tomorrow at three-fifteen, ready to work."

"Thanks, coach," said Stephanie, practically jumping for joy. He thought she was good! He wanted to get her in the intramurals! It was too much! It was terrific!

Stephanie ran most of the way home. She was charged with a new sense of purpose. Maybe this is what kept Alex going full steam all the time. Knowing she was good. And knowing she could prove it. Stephanie slowed to a walk up the front walk. Better hang on, she warned herself. You've only had one lesson. You haven't proven anything yet.

"Steph, that you?" called Alex from the back porch.

"Yes . . . wait till I tell you," replied Stephanie excitedly. She rushed around the house, toward the back, then slid to a halt, all her blood draining instantly to her toes. Rick was sitting on the chair next to Alex.

Stephanie looked from Alex to Rick and back to Alex. Darn Alex! She'd probably invited Rick over.

trying to control Stephanie's life again. Why didn't she mind her own business?

"Uh... I didn't realize you had company," said Stephanie, "Catch you later."

"No, Steph, Rick came to see you. Here, have some lemonade. I just made it." She poured Stephanie a glass.

Rick took her arm and led her over to the swing. "Please, Steph, I want to talk to you."

Stephanie felt like a caged bird. Her heart was banging wildly against her ribs. Well, if they had to have a confrontation, they might as well get it over with. She couldn't keep sneaking around in the halls avoiding him forever. She sat down.

"Look, Stephanie," said Rick taking her hands. His touch sent a bolt of electricity through her. She looked down. His fingers were lean and strong and tanned, making hers seem extra pale and delicate in comparison. She felt a lump in her throat.

"I want to apologize for Saturday," he continued.

Stephanie looked up in confusion. What was he apologizing for? She'd started everything by being such a jerk. She should have been able to deal with that wedding scene better. After all, she'd weathered worse than that before—explaining why you'd stolen a pack of cigarettes to some gray-haired old judge was a lot tougher than facing a bunch of rich nerds. She should have laughed it off.

"Hey, look," she said, standing up and letting go of Rick's hands. She stared out across the yard and stuffed her hands in the pockets of her shorts.

"That was Saturday... this is Monday. Let's forget it, huh? I survived."

"But I wanted us to have a good time...a really good time, and I blew it. I guess I was kind of wound up, but it's not every day your sister gets married. I was pretty excited about the whole thing. I forgot that you wouldn't know anyone there and might feel uncomfortable about being thrown into a group of strangers. I should have stayed with you. I want you to know I feel really bad about that."

"I said, forget it," repeated Stephanie, trying to keep a hard edge to her voice. Why couldn't she just turn around and apologize, too? After all, he'd taken the first step. But even if she did, what sort of future would they have? The lies wouldn't change. They couldn't. She could never tell him about her past now. Saturday had merely emphasized how vastly different their lives and backgrounds really were. That idea that they could find a common ground was pure fantasy. Rick was better off without her. She had to make him see that, no matter how painful it was. Otherwise they were going to destroy each other.

"Stephanie, listen to me," he said with rising frustration. "We said some pretty nasty things to each other. I'm here to apologize for my part. I'm here to get things back to where they were before all this. I ...I miss you."

Stephanie knew that she would burst into tears if she tried to say anything, so she concentrated on the big cottonwood tree in the backyard, counting its leaves, trying to imagine how old it was.

"Darn it, Steph! Say something...anything, or do you truly not care about what happens to our relationship? Where's all that fighting spirit I admire so much in you. Huh? Answer me!" He paused. "Tell me you'll go to the Spring Fling with me."

The Spring Fling! Stephanie felt as if she'd been thrown across the room. Next to the prom, it was the biggest dance of the semester. And, after all she'd put him through, he still wanted her to go with him? For the first time, Stephanie realized how much Rick was a fighter, too.

Her chest burned with imprisoned emotion. Oh, to let it out; to throw her arms around him and let it all out. But she couldn't. She couldn't go on living the lies but she didn't see how she could possibly tell him the truth either. If she really loved Rick, she'd set him free. Stephanie wrenched her mind away from Rick and forced herself to concentrate on the tree. It must be 200 years old—at least 200 years. Maybe more. That means it was here during the gold rush. Indians probably camped under it. Rick's grandfather might have paused in its shade while looking for a spot to build his home.

"Okay, Steph, I get the message...finally. You must think I'm pretty slow. Actually, I just couldn't bear giving you up without a fight. You're worth that much to me." She heard the grating of his chair as he stood up. He was leaving. Her anguish was unbearable—the pain so acute, she felt physically sick. Still she didn't look at him. "I'm sorry things ended up this way. I thought we had more going for us. Obviously I was wrong. Kirk Wallace and his illegal weapons seem to hold more fascination for you, don't they?" Rick paused. "Well, have fun. See you around."

Stephanie waited until she heard the front door

slam before she moved. Then she sank to the floor and burst into tears.

Stephanie's heart missed a beat when she saw the note sticking out of her locker the next day. Rick? Please no. She was only so strong.

"Dear Stephanie," the note read. "Come down to KA this afternoon if you can. We have a possible lead. Bruce."

Stephanie quickly ripped the note into a million pieces while her heart went crazy. A lead on her mother! Maybe they'd located her! Maybe she'd walk into Room 404 this afternoon and there would sit—her mother! All her problems would be solved then.

"Hi, guys," sang out Stephanie as she floated up to the lunch table several hours later. "How's it going?"

Everyone looked up at her in surprise, then exchanged glances. Stephanie didn't care. Nothing, absolutely nothing could dampen her euphoria right now. In less than four hours she'd be speaking with her mother, breaking a twelve-year silence.

"Hi, Steph," they all replied hesitantly.

"Nice day, huh?"

"Nice? Nice if you like forty-five degrees and overcast, or haven't you noticed spring shipped out overnight? If it doesn't get warm soon I swear I'm going to hibernate—go to bed and refuse to get up until July."

Stephanie laughed. "It's still a great day, clouds and all."

"You do kind of look like you won the Irish Sweepstakes," Alex remarked. "Did you and Rick manage to patch things up last night?"

Dark clouds descended immediately, but Stephanie pushed them back determinedly, as she sat down next to Lori and unwrapped her cheese sandwich. The only way she could survive the pain of losing Rick was not to think about him.

"Let's just say things are resolved," said Stephanie quietly.

"I'm so glad," said Lori. "It can be so painful when you don't communicate."

"Steph, Alex told us what happened Saturday," broke in Elaine. "We're really sorry you had to go through all that."

"People can be so insensitive sometimes, it's hard to believe," Kit added.

"Aw . . . thanks, gang," said Stephanie, embarrassed but warmed by their support. "But that's all over."

She glanced around at the faces surrounding her. This group had really given her a lot of breaks. She'd never find another batch of friends like this. Never. And now maybe she was about to lose them—if she went to live with her mother. Of course, her mother might not live that far away. And they could all visit. Have sleepovers. Meet at the beach for picnics. It wouldn't be the same, but at least they'd all still be friends. Hurriedly Stephanie finished her lunch, then rushed off to find Bruce.

Stephanie bounded up the steps to Room 404 two at a time. She hadn't found Bruce at lunch, so she didn't know any more details than the note that morning.

"Ah, Steph. Great. You're here," said Bruce, his face breaking out in a smile excitedly when she pushed through the door. "I've just been on the phone following leads."

"Yeah! Did you find her?" asked Stephanie breathlessly. "Is she coming in today?"

"Whoa . . . whoa." Bruce laughed. "I only said we had a lead, a clue. But it looks like it might be something. Here's the scoop. We've located a woman who lives about fifty miles away . . . in Santa Maria del Mar."

"Oh, then I would be changing schools," said Stephanie, torn by the news.

"Steph," said Bruce gently, putting his arm around her shoulders "Don't jump ahead of the facts. We don't even know if this is your mother. But we have a Corrie Burroughs who gave up a child . . . a five-year-old girl . . . twelve years ago. That's all we have to go on, and we had to piece that together from a zillion fragments."

"So what do we do now?" asked Stephanie.

"We were waiting for you, then we thought we'd call her. What do you say? Are you ready for this?"

"Ready! Bruce, I'm going nuts. Let's go!"

"Okay. Why don't you go pick up the extension in the other room. I'll call from in here. When we're certain it's your mom, you take over."

"Great," said Stephanie, rushing next door. With shaking hands she picked up the receiver and listened to Bruce dial the number. It rang once, then again. Stephanie's mouth was dry, her stomach knotted with anxiety. On the third ring, someone answered.

"Yeah," said a rough female voice. Stephanie was taken aback but controlled herself. Maybe this was her mother's maid or something.

"Yes... Mrs. Burroughs?" asked Bruce politely. "Is this Mrs. Corrie Burroughs?"

"Yeah. What do ya want?"

Stephanie felt a wave of nausea wash over her. It was all she could do to hold the phone to her ear. This didn't sound like the beautiful mother she'd imagined with the melodic voice.

"I wanted to ask you a few questions, Mrs. Burroughs," continued Bruce.

"You aren't selling something, are you?" growled Mrs. Burroughs. "Because if you are, forget it! I'm not buying, ya hear?"

"No, Mrs. Burroughs, I'm Bruce Fletcher and I work for an agency that helps orphans find their real parents. I've been looking for my own parents for two years."

There was a pause, then, "What's it to me?"

"Well, my client Stephanie Burroughs is looking for her mother. She's seventeen and her mother gave her up when she was five."

"Young man, I don't care what you are or who you're looking for, but if you ever disturb me again, I'll call the police."

Stephanie could feel panic rising inside her. "Mother!" she called into the receiver. "Mother... please."

"Listen, kid, I'm not your mother—I never had a daughter. And, young man, get your facts straight next time. It was a boy I gave up twelve years ago, not a girl." The phone went dead. Stephanie stared at it a moment, then burst into tears. Bruce was at her side in a flash, his arms around her.

"Oh, Stephanie, I'm so sorry," he said, hugging her as she cried. "I'm so, so sorry."

"You can't blame yourself, Bruce," Stephanie sobbed. "You tried. You really tried. I'm very thankful for that."

"And we'll keep trying," he said gently. "I promise."

Chapter Eight

"Alex, you're really good," Stephanie said hesitantly. "I mean . . . your diving. I was impressed."

"Aw . . . well," mumbled Alex, turning on the TV and flopping down on the sofa beside Stephanie. They were both exhausted: Alex from the big swim meet that afternoon and Stephanie from her tennis. She'd cut her lesson short to go watch Alex, but it had been worth it. What a show!

"I could be much better, though," continued Alex, "My second twist was a bit sloppy on that last dive."

"Sloppy! The crowd went nuts when you pulled that off," exclaimed Stephanie. "And the man next to me said you were the only one in the whole region who did that dive. No wonder you won."

"I've still got a long way to go if I'm going to make

the Olympic team."

"Alex, give yourself a break! At least you're on your way. What more do you want?"

"Well, speaking of being on the way," said Alex evasively, "Cathy Marden—her sister's on the swim team with me—said you're one hotshot tennis player."

Stephanie's cheeks reddened. "I think that's stretching it. But it's fun."

"Well, she said the coach is grooming you as his secret weapon in the intramurals. That sounds pretty good to me."

"Aw . . . I think he just feels sorry for me since I'm probably the only senior at Glenwood High who doesn't know how to play tennis."

"Come on, Steph. Give yourself a break. Admit it—you're good. Right?"

"Only if you admit you're the best diver in the region, maybe even the state," shot back Stephanie. "Admit it, Alex! Admit it!"

And then they were laughing. Laughing so hard Stephanie fell off the sofa and rolled on the floor.

"Geez, I hope nobody heard us," she cried, wiping her eyes.

"What a couple of jerks we are," giggled Alex, holding her sides. "Can you believe us?"

"Admit it, admit it," repeated Stephanie, bursting out with renewed laughter. "We sounded like a couple of five-year-olds."

"Or sisters . . . " said Alex, helping Stephanie back up onto the sofa.

"That's what sisters sound like?" asked Stephanie.

"I guess so," Alex replied. "We're sisters and that's exactly what we sounded like."

Stephanie glanced quickly away. She still found it hard to believe that Alex really considered her a sister. "Boy, we sure are stubborn, though."

"Yeah, I never knew there was anyone as stubborn as I am" — Alex giggled — "until you moved in. But I still think I have you beat."

"Ha!" retorted Stephanie. "One time I didn't eat for three days because my foster parents said I couldn't go to a sleepover. Beat that!"

"Well," said Alex thoughtfully. "When my parents wouldn't let me get a car, I went around honking every time they talked to me."

Stephanie giggled. "You didn't."

"I did. For a whole week." Both girls cracked up again.

"Remember Mrs. Greenspan at the Crestview Home for Girls?" asked Stephanie.

"Ugh, do I ever. The bride of Dracula."

"You got it. Well, when she told me not to smoke in my room, I snuck around, emptying every ashtray in the whole place, and filled my room with butts. She flipped out. I mean it was the first time I ever saw her lose her cool."

Alex laughed. "I'd have loved to have seen that."

"And then one time I hitchhiked all the way to L.A. and back in twenty-four hours on a dare," said Stephanie.

"Okay. Okay. You've got me beat. You win, but you've got to admit I run a close second."

"Yeah, I'll give you that," Stephanie acknowledged.

"Hey, here comes our movie," said Alex, adjusting the volume on the TV. The credits for *The Sound of Music* were just rolling up.

"My favorite," sighed Stephanie.

"Me, too," said Alex. "Before it starts, what do you say we get something to eat?"

"Sounds good to me," said Stephanie, taking off for the kitchen. They were back in two seconds flat, Stephanie with the crackers and a knife, Alex with the jar of peanut butter.

An hour later, when the song "Climb Every Mountain" began, Stephanie sighed. "Oh, I love this part," she whispered and then joined in, singing softly, lost in the beautiful words telling her to try everything until she found her dream.

When the song ended, she saw that Alex was staring at her in awe. "You have an amazing voice," said Alex, "really amazing."

"Huh?... Oh," stammered Stephanie. She'd almost forgotten about Alex, so lost had she been in the song. It always inspired her. Like sunsets. That song made her want to believe in things again. "Thanks."

"Yeah, you should be singing in the chorus. Glenwood's got one of the best in the state. They even cut a record last year."

"Yeah?" Stephanie replied. She loved to sing. She used to sing a lot when she was alone. Somehow it made her feel closer to her mother. But she'd never had the nerve to sing in public. In grade school all her music teachers used to go nuts because she never joined in.

"Yeah."

After that, the girls sang the familiar words of every song that came up, laughing when they missed the lyrics and sometimes changing the words around just to be silly. But at the end of the movie, when Captain von Trapp came out on the stage and sang "Edelweiss," they sat quietly listening.

When the final credits came on the screen, Alex ran a paper towel over her nose, trying to hide her sniffles. "What a great movie," she said softly.

"Too bad real life doesn't always work out so well," Stephanie replied, coughing loudly. A tear slid off her cheek and made a dark blue patch on her faded jeans.

"Are you crying?" asked Alex.

Stephanie took a deep breath to control herself. "Over a dumb movie? Ha! You must be kidding. Are you?"

"Naw," said Alex quickly, blowing her nose loudly.

All at once Stephanie giggled, but it caught in her throat and came out as a sob. "Are we being stubborn again?"

Alex looked at Stephanie, tears standing out in her eyes. "It looks like it."

Stephanie hiccupped in reply, and the two girls fell into each other's arms, laughing.

Finally Alex got up and began picking up their plates. "I can almost forgive Wes all his craziness after seeing that."

"I know what you mean," said Stephanie. "Now I wish I were going to the Spring Fling with Rick."

"You mean you're not?" exclaimed Alex.

"No, not after you told him why I left the wedding.

I don't need anyone feeling sorry for me."

"After I did what?" cried Alex.

"That day I came home and found you two on the porch . . ."

"He'd only been there two seconds. Okay. Okay. Maybe three seconds," protested Alex.

"You mean . . . you didn't . . . tell him everything I'd told you?"

"Of course not," cried Alex indignantly. "What kind of friend do you think I am? All I did was offer him a glass of lemonade."

"But didn't you invite him over here in the first place?" demanded Stephanie.

"Stephanie, you really think I'm an ogre. So, okay, I screwed up a couple of times when you first came, trying to get you dates and everything, but I don't do that anymore."

"Geez, I'm really sorry, Alex," said Stephanie quietly. "You mean he came over 'cause he really wanted to see me?"

"Sure, dummy. Why is that so hard to believe? The guy's nuts about you. Anyone can see that."

"Yeah? You think so?" asked Stephanie, her heart swelling. "You really think so?"

"Of course I do. Why don't you call him up and tell him you've changed your mind and would love to go to the dance after all."

Stephanie felt weak all over. "No, I couldn't do that."

"Why not?" demanded Alex.

"I just couldn't, that's all."

"Then why not come with Wes and me? I know Rick is going to be there. He was in front of me in line at the ticket booth today."

"Oh," said Stephanie, sagging with disappointment, despite herself. "That probably means he has a date."

"He bought *one* ticket," replied Alex triumphantly. "*Uno.* Get it? He's going stag."

"Well, maybe I should . . ." Maybe she'd been wrong. Maybe they could make it work out. After all, wasn't everything supposed to work out somehow if two people liked each other?

"Of course you should. The dance would be a nice neutral territory where you guys could talk things out."

"That's true. Things have gotten kind of screwy, that's for sure." Stephanie cleared her throat. "You and Wes wouldn't mind me tagging along?"

"We'd love it," cried Alex. "Besides, Wes will still be on crutches then, so I'll be mostly sitting there, playing nurse all evening."

"Thanks, Alex," said Stephanie.

"Aw . . ." said Alex, "it's nothing."

"Alex . . ."

Alex laughed. "I'm doing it again, right?"

"Right."

Both girls cracked up.

Stephanie let out her breath slowly as she looked around the gym the next evening. Saturday night at Glenwood High, and the senior class was ready to party! The decorations committee had done a great job. With the Gatsby era as their theme, they'd draped the whole ceiling with striped material so that it resembled a large summer tent. At one end of the gym, on a raised platform, the band was playing a Prince song, and there was a fountain in the middle of the floor spurting real water. Everyone had been asked to come in white, so the scene floated before Stephanie's eyes like a shimmering mirage.

But it was obvious she was the only one without a date. Couples who weren't dancing were seated on the white iron benches dotted about, or hovering over the refreshment table. Stephanie spotted Ginger and Craig, who looked like a piece of sculpture, so intently were they staring into each other's eyes. Stephanie waved to Elaine and Carl, and Kit and Justin were lost in the romantic world around them and didn't see her. Elaine looked really beautiful in a high-collared, light cotton Victorian dress with her dark hair piled loosely on top of her head. Most of the girls had come in Victorian style, making the whole gym look like a big Ralph Lauren ad. The vintage clothing shops of the area must have bare shelves tonight, mused Stephanie, letting her eye wander slowly over the scene. Kit looked a little funkier in a flowing white harem outfit. She had a bright turquoise ribbon tied saucily in her mop of curls and matching turquoise slippers.

"Wow! This is really neat," said Alex. She looked . . . well . . . typically Alex in her genuine 1930s baggy linen trousers, suspenders, and striped shirt and bow tie. Only Alex could carry off an outfit like that, thought Stephanie, and still look totally feminine — even chic.

"Yeah." Stephanie sighed, wishing she were sharing it all with someone special . . . like Rick.

Wes hopped athletically over to the table and settled easily back in a chair. His longish dark curls were damp from the effort of the crutches, but his light green eyes sparkled devilishly. "Here I have the two best-looking dates in the whole joint, and all I can do is watch you have fun. Now that's a bummer."

Alex laughed. "Listen to the old man. Two days ago you were complaining about being dragged off to my teeny-bopper world."

"Well, you've got to admit, my age and sophistication make me stand out in a place like this," he joked.

"Kind of like a sore thumb," quipped Alex, giving him a quick kiss on the cheek. "Or, considering your profession, maybe I should say a 'fifth wheel.' But don't worry, I'm not going to leave you to the wolves. I'm so stiff from playing tennis with Stephanie all morning, I don't think I could dance anyway."

"You might be stiff," said Stephanie, "but you beat the pants off me."

"Sorry I missed the match," joked Wes, and Alex gave him a playful punch.

"Cool it, big boy, you don't look too tough right now stumbling around on those crutches." She laughed. "Besides, I didn't beat the pants off Steph. I had to work for every point I got."

"Well, let's just say you worked very hard and made lots of points," giggled Stephanie. "At least they added up to a lot more than I had."

"Yeah, but you're good, Steph—and getting better all the time. Watch out, Marcia Connors!"

"What do you mean?" Stephanie asked.

"You'll be playing Marcia in the intramurals. She always enters."

"Oh, no," groaned Stephanie. "I shouldn't have

signed up."

"Of course you should have. It's time someone took Marcia down a couple of notches. She thinks she's sooooo good."

"But why does that someone have to be me?" said Stephanie. "Couldn't you just throw me into the lion's den at the San Francisco Zoo. I think I'd have an easier time."

Alex and Wes laughed.

"Let's just say that's what we have in mind if you don't beat her," joked Alex.

Stephanie rolled her eyes, then turned to watch the dancers. She couldn't deny that the idea of beating Marcia Connors at tennis appealed to her. But how long had Marcia been playing tennis? What were her four measly weeks of training compared to years of work?

"Steph," said Alex in a loud whisper. "There's Rick! By the punch bowl."

Stephanie was sure her heart stopped beating for a moment. Rick looked devastatingly handsome in baggy white trousers and shirt and a pale green tie. He'd just had a haircut, which made him look younger, less sophisticated. He was entertaining a group of people around him; the girls were practically eating out of his hand, and every once in a while they'd all roar with laughter. It didn't look as though he was with anyone special, though. Stephanie's hopes rose.

"Go on," urged Alex.

"Too many people," Stephanie replied.

"So what," Alex shot back. "You're certainly not going to resolve anything sitting here drooling over him, are you?"

Alex was right. It was time to go for it. She wanted Rick Forrester. That's all there was to it. If she had to crawl on her knees to get him back, then crawl she would. Stephanie took a deep breath and walked over.

"Hi . . . uh . . . Rick," she said, her knees knocking together under the skirt of the white eyelet dress Lori had lent her. Mrs. Enomoto had said she looked very pretty and sweet. Stephanie wasn't sure she wanted to look sweet, but her hair, hanging long and loose, gave her a cloak to hide behind.

"Steph! You're here! You came after all! How wonderful!"

Stephanie felt herself relax a bit. At least he was glad to see her.

"Rick . . . I . . . I want to apolo—" began Stephanie.

"Richard, quick! This is absolutely the most divine song. You promised me this dance, anyway." Marcia Connors materialized out of nowhere, it seemed, and dragged Rick onto the dance floor without even a glance at Stephanie.

Stephanie turned and fled into the coatroom, not daring to look back. A huge sob escaped from her as she burrowed deep into the racks, but immediately she stifled it. More people were coming into the room. Stephanie slid in between two stacks of lightweight jackets and coats to stay hidden until they'd gone.

"You know," said one voice, "I think Stephanie Burroughs just throws herself at Rick Forrester."

"Can't she see she doesn't have a chance?" said another. "Doesn't she know?"

"I can't imagine she doesn't. You can see the ring he gave Marcia from a mile away."

"And a ring can only mean one thing, right?"

"Marcia said they were going to keep it secret for a while, though."

"If I were going steady with a hunk like Rick Forrester I'd probably take out a full-page ad in the newspaper."

Stephanie was biting her hand to keep from crying out. Each of their words was like another knife finding its way to her already shattered heart.

Finally they wandered back out, and Stephanie was left alone with her grief. Going steady! Marcia and Rick were going steady? He'd given her a ring? Stephanie didn't know how long she stayed slumped against the wall, but it seemed like forever.

Finally she grabbed her jacket and swung it defiantly over her shoulder. *Well, fine,* she thought angrily, yanking open the door. *Marcia can have him. I don't need him. I don't need anybody.*

Chapter Nine

"Hey, Steph, where're you going?"

Stephanie turned to see Bruce approaching.

"I'm splitting," she said hotly.

"Gosh, things are just starting to warm up. How about a dance? Gayle's in the girls' room, and knowing her she'll be there for a long time." He grinned good-naturedly.

"Thanks anyway, but I've had enough of this scene. I might puke if I have to stay any longer."

"Is something wrong, Steph?" Bruce put his hand gently on her arm, his smile instantly fading. "Want to talk about it?"

Stephanie felt herself weaken. Bruce knew where she was coming from. If ony she could relax and tell him about it. They'd probably find some way to turn it into a big joke. But beyond Bruce she could see Marcia Connors dancing with Rick, the dim light glinting off a beautiful gold ring on her left hand.

"Naw . . . I gotta go," she said with renewed determination. "Thanks anyway, Bruce." She headed out the door to the parking lot, Bruce at her heels.

"Please, Steph. I know you're upset. I can feel it. Talk to me."

Tears stung her eyes. She hesitated, then shook her head angrily. She said she didn't need anyone. Now she was going to prove it.

"Well, hello, princess. Where's the ball?"

Stephanie froze. She'd been so angry she hadn't noticed she'd walked smack into the middle of Kirk Wallace and his friends, lounging on their cars, drinking beer. At least the others were—Kirk looked sober.

"Stephanie, I don't think you should get mixed up with this crowd," begged Bruce from behind. "I'll take you home, if that's what you want. Let me just get the keys from Gayle."

"I can look after myself, okay?" shot back Stephanie. She didn't want to ruin his evening, too. "Hey, Kirk, wanna do me a favor and give me a ride home?"

A roar of approval rose from the boys around Kirk.

"Hey, man, if you don't want her, send her my way," yelled one.

"Lady Luck is smiling down on Old Kirk tonight, huh?" said another.

Stephanie's legs felt weak, and her cheeks were burning, but she kept looking Kirk straight in the eye.

"What's the matter, babe, the action get too hot and heavy for you in there?" He swaggered over to her. "Sure I'll give you a ride. Hop in."

Stephanie jumped in without waiting for a second invitation. She didn't even wave to Bruce as they spun out of the parking lot.

"Listen to that engine," said Kirk. "Purring like a cat. I've been working on it all day. New overhead cam."

Stephanie remembered the days when she used to love to talk engines, just to prove how cool she was. But tonight, talking about a new overhead cam was about as boring as she could imagine. She wanted to get home, to go to sleep, and forget the nightmare of her life.

"Let me show you what it'll do," said Kirk, turning up Main Street and away from town.

"Kirk, I'm really tired. Please just take me home," said Stephanie wearily.

"Hey . . . look, I'm going out of my way for you, so you can be nice to me. Okay? I'm going to show you one mean engine . . . and you're going to like it." He stomped on the accelerator, and Stephanie was flattened against the back of the seat. Gasping with fear, she watched the speedometer climb—60, 70, 80 miles per hour.

"Kirk, watch out!" she screamed as he peeled through a red light, barely missing a car. "Slow down! You're going to get us killed."

He threw back his head and laughed, and Stephanie realized with horror that Kirk had neither forgotten nor forgiven her rejection of his suit. "Relax, babe, I'm in control now. You have nothing to fear."

"Kirk, let me out this minute!" demanded Stephanie, her panic growing. "I mean it. Stop this car! I'd rather walk."

"Would you, now?" Kirk said sarcastically. "But I haven't even kicked in the overhead cam yet. Watch this."

Stephanie's heart rose higher and higher in her throat as the needle of the speedometer continued to climb.

Suddenly Kirk snarled. "I think we've got some pigs on our tail."

Stephanie felt weak with relief. At least the cops could stop Kirk and get her safely home. She almost laughed out loud. She never thought she'd see the day when she was glad to see cops. Most of her life had been spent running from them.

"Well, no pig's gonna take Kirk Wallace. Not in this machine. No way." Kirk floored the accelerator again, and the car lurched forward.

"Darn it, Kirk, stop it!" demanded Stephanie. "Kill yourself, but not me."

"I said relax, babe."

They were headed north on the coast road now. Stephanie knew that there were mountains to the right and steep cliffs leading down to the beach on the left. One false move, and it could all be over. She cringed as the car squealed around the winding corners, leaving patches of rubber in the straightaways.

"You've pushed me to the limit. Well now I'm going to push you. Leading me on, teasing me, then pulling back—'Oh, no, Kirk, I'm not interested in you *that* way,'" he said, mimicking Stephanie in a high, unnatural voice. "Let me see you beg now."

"Come on, Kirk, grow up—we've had enough, don't you think?" pleaded Stephanie, her knuckles white where she gripped the door handle. Her feet were jammed against the front of the car to keep herself from being thrown around in the seat. "Someone's going to get hurt."

"Well, it's not going to be me, babe. I promise you that."

Stephanie glanced over at him. The lights from the car behind bounced off the rearview mirror and were reflected in his glazed eyes. She had to do something, but her mind and body were paralyzed with fear. Kirk was completely out of control.

The tires screamed again in protest. Louder this time. An agonized, almost human sound that raked Stephanie's brain warned her that her life was on the line.

"Kirk!" she managed to yell as the landscape suddenly spun crazily around in the beam of headlights. There was sky, then cliff, then the road coming off at a weird angle. Time slowed down . . . and Stephanie felt herself tumbling . . . slowly . . . over, crashing into things . . . hard things, sharp things, all over her body . . . all the while the horrible crunching and squealing sound continued its loud concert. And then . . . there was nothing. The noises stopped, and Stephanie felt as if she were falling down a black, bottomless well. She put her hands out to break a fall that never seemed to come.

"Steph . . . Stephanie, can you hear me?"

At first Stephanie thought she was home in bed. Was it morning already? She still felt so tired and couldn't seem to open her eyes. She strained and strained, but they remained closed. She tried to move her body, but it wouldn't respond. Finally she sagged back on her pillow with a moan.

"It's okay, Steph. Just take it easy. There's no rush."

The voice floated over her like a balm. Then a cool hand brushed her forehead. "When you can, say something to me. Anything."

What a strange command, thought Stephanie, her fuzzy mind working to understand what was going on. She moved her mouth, trying to follow orders, trying to say something. Everything hurt.

"Good morning," she mumbled.

A soft laugh that was almost a cry sounded close to her ear. "Thank God you're alive!" The voice was familiar, but Stephanie couldn't quite place it. She felt herself being rocked gently back and forth. Now she was sure she wasn't in her bed, but where was she? Who was this person holding her? With a huge effort, Stephanie opened her eyes.

Rick! Rick's face was bent over her tenderly, and she realized with a start that she was lying beside the road, her head cradled in his lap. Rick had tears in his eyes, even though he was smiling. Stephanie tried to smile back.

"Where am I?" she asked.

"You've been in a very bad car accident," said Rick, smoothing her hair back from her forehead. "But you're okay. Everything's okay now."

Stephanie closed her eyes again. The gravel dug sharply into her back. The cool night air fanned her into full consciousness. Then she remembered. Kirk and the coast road and the terrible noise. The crash.

She opened her eyes again and looked around. The car lay twenty yards off, its wheels in the air. It was a gruesome, unnatural sight.

"How's Kirk?" she mumbled. "Is he . . . is he . . . ?"

"He's alive. He's fine." Rick's voice was bitter. "He almost killed you both, though."

"But we're okay?" asked Stephanie.

"I think so," Rick replied gently. "Why don't you move your arms and legs—easy now—and tell me if anything hurts."

He supported Stephanie in his arms while she cautiously moved one arm, then the other, then her legs.

"Whew! Everything seems okay," reported Rick, then buried his head in her neck. "Oh, Steph, I'm so glad you're alive. I thought . . . I thought . . . I mean when I saw that car flip around like that—you went over twice—I thought you were dead." He squeezed her gently and kissed her tenderly all over the face. Tears of relief stood out in his eyes. Stephanie reached up and brushed them away, her eyes stinging with her own tears.

Suddenly the lights of a car splashed over them, making the wreckage seem like a bizarre piece of sculpture in a floodlit exhibit.

"Can I help? Is everyone all right here?" said a voice, and a man stepped into the ring of light. "I'm a doctor."

"Thank goodness," said Rick. "I think everything's okay, Doctor . . ."

"Mallory. I have a practice in Palo Alto."

"I've checked them both out and nothing seems to be obviously wrong, but I remember from a first aid course that internal bleeding can be a problem. Can you take a look at them while you're here, please?"

"Them?" asked Dr. Mallory.

"Yes, there's a boy on the other side of the car . . . in the ditch."

The doctor examined Stephanie, then went over to Kirk.

"No external injuries, except for a few cuts and bruises," the doctor told Rick when he came back. "But to be safe, I recommend that you take them to the hospital to get examined for shock and possible internal injuries." He turned to Stephanie. "And I'd get an ice pack on your head as soon as possible, young lady. You're going to have a prize-winning bump up there as it is."

Stephanie smiled weakly. "Okay, Doc."

"From the looks of that car," the doctor continued, "you two are mighty lucky. People don't usually walk away from an accident like that." Stephanie nodded, clutching Rick's hand tightly. Gently Rick wrapped his coat around her shoulders, just as a police car screamed up the road and swung in beside them.

Darn, thought Stephanie. *Someone must have passed the wreck and alerted the cops. Just what we don't need.*

The cop and doctor conferred briefly, then the doctor left and the cop sauntered over.

"I'll take care of this," whispered Rick, escorting Stephanie back to his car. "There'll be a bunch of routine questions for the accident report. That's all. You try to keep warm."

Stephanie slumped against Rick's car. She was

exhausted, and her whole body was beginning to ache. Through glassy eyes she watched Rick and the cop talk, then go over and question Kirk who was now sitting dejectedly beside his trashed car. He looked like a wounded, defeated animal. Gone was every ounce of bravado. As angry as she was at Kirk for his reckless, stupid behavior, her heart went out to him. She remembered all the times when life had defeated her and there was no one around to pick up the pieces. It was tough always facing your mistakes on your own.

Finally the cop came over and asked her to make a statement on the accident. Stephanie just gave him the bare facts, trying to make it appear as if it really had been an accident—a grease patch on the road, for instance—that caused them to go over. She didn't mention how fast Kirk was going or his angry state of mind.

"Well, I've got about all I need," said the cop, flipping his notebook closed and casting his eye over the scene once more. "I've called for a wrecker from Scotty's garage over in Palo Alto, so that'll be here soon. You kids can go on home or to the hospital now, but I want you to show up at the station tomorrow at ten to make a complete report. I'll charge you then." He hesitated. "Want me to take the cowboy?" he asked, nodding toward Kirk.

His sarcastic tone grated on Stephanie's nerves. She glared up at him.

"Sure . . ." began Rick, but Stephanie cut him off.

"No," she said firmly. "We'll take care of him ourselves. Thanks, anyway."

The cop hesitated, looking from Rick to Stephanie.

"Well, if you're certain . . ." he said. "I'll be going. Remember. Ten sharp. Tomorrow."

"We'll be there, officer," said Rick still staring at Stephanie in confusion. "Thanks for everything."

"Why did you do that?" asked Rick when the cop had driven off.

"I just don't think Kirk needs some cop hassling him any more tonight," said Stephanie defensively, limping over to Kirk. Feebly he smiled his thanks up at her. Maybe if the world showed Kirk a little kindness for once, he'd see it wasn't such a bad place. Maybe. Besides, if she didn't help him out, there was no telling what he might do.

"Well, I hope you have a better explanation than that, Stephanie," Rick said flatly. "And I mean to hear it. No more game playing. No more clamming up and refusing to talk. Okay?"

"Okay," said Stephanie, slipping into the car. "But I don't want to go to the hospital—I don't need to, all right?"

Kirk asked Rick to take him directly home, too, and the three of them drove back down the winding road in silence. Closing her eyes, Stephanie tried not to think about anything. Her body throbbed with pain. Kirk lay silently in the small section behind the front seats.

They found Kirk's house down past the Kids Anonymous building, on a street filled with potholes and ill-kept houses.

"I'll get him in," said Stephanie, sliding gingerly out her door and helping Kirk. He leaned heavily on her as she walked him up the rickety front steps. Stephanie had to kick the door with her foot because her hands were too scratched to knock.

"Yeah . . . who is it?" came a gruff voice from within.

"Stephanie Burroughs, Mr. Wallace," called out Stephanie. "I've got Kirk with me. He's been in an accident."

The door flew open and a large, unshaven man peered out. He shook his head. "I kept telling that darn kid he was going to hurt himself one day. Well, it looks like he's done a right good job of it."

"Mr. Wallace," Stephanie spoke up firmly. "Kirk doesn't need a hard time. I don't think anything's broken, but he needs your help."

Mr. Wallace looked from Stephanie to Kirk. Finally he put his arm around Kirk's shoulders.

"Come on in, son," he said in a different tone of voice. "I'll look after you. We'll have you fixed up in no time." He led Kirk gently through the door, then turned to Stephanie. His features were soft and defenseless. "Thanks, Miss. Thanks a lot for helping my boy."

Rick was strangely quiet on the ride over to the Enomotos'. The house was empty. It was only ten o'clock. Everyone was still out for the evening. Rick helped her in, then put on a pan of milk after opening practically every cupboard in the kitchen looking for everything. Stephanie wanted to help him, but she felt drained and shaky and incapable of logical thinking.

"I think you should have a hot shower, then put on something warm," said Rick. "You've had a horrible experience. I don't want you to go into shock or anything like that. I'll have this chocolate ready by the time you get down—and an ice pack."

Stephanie wanted to throw her arms around him. She was so thankful for his strong, capable presence. But something held her back. Something in his eyes. She limped upstairs and followed his orders, letting the warm water wash over her whole body in a comforting stream. Soon she stopped shivering uncontrollably and began to relax. Afterward she slipped into a snuggly blue sweatsuit and quickly ran a comb through her wet hair.

When she came down, the kitchen seemed like a haven of warmth and security after the nightmare of her evening. There were the familiar plants and the checked tablecloth...and Rick handing her a steaming mug of chocolate. Had she really been lying on the hard gravel road just over an hour ago wondering if she were dead or alive? She fingered the rising bump on her head gingerly. A shudder rushed through her from top to bottom, shaking the very core of her existence. It suddenly hit her how lucky she was to be alive. Rick helped her to a chair at the table and placed her mug beside her. Stephanie smiled weakly.

"Steph," he said seriously, sitting down. "I want to ask you something."

"Yeah?" she said, slowly sipping her chocolate with one hand, holding the ice pack in place with the other. She could feel the chocolate's warmth begin to soothe the final aches in her body, and the cool ice immediately numbed the throbbing in her head.

"How can you be so nice to that jerk Wallace, even after he almost kills you? I just don't understand it."

Stephanie tried to keep her hands from shaking.

To explain why she was nice to Kirk meant explaining how and why she understood the world they shared. She glanced across the table at him, her eyes wide with fear.

"Are you interested in Kirk?" coaxed Rick gently. "Is that it?"

Stephanie shook her head slowly.

"Has he threatened you?"

Again Stephanie shook her head.

"Stephanie, if you care for me at all, please try to explain this to me. I want to understand you so badly." He reached across the table and took her hand.

Stephanie burst into tears. "Oh, Rick, what's the use? What's the use?" The kitchen was quiet except for the sounds of her sobbing.

"Because...because I...I love you, Stephanie," whispered Rick. "That's why."

Another wave of anguish broke over her, and sobs racked her slender frame anew. Rick came around to her side and pulled a chair over so he could wrap her in his arms.

"I'm sorry," he said, kissing her forehead tenderly. "I was an idiot for bringing this up now, after all you've been through. Forgive me."

"Rick," sobbed Stephanie, "you have every right to bring it up. I've been screwing around with your life for too long. It's time I leveled with you."

Strange, but even that small admission made her feel better. How she'd hated all the lies. She took a deep breath and sat up to face him.

"Kirk and I understand each other," she began.

"You understand that selfish jerk?" said Rick, his

voice rising slightly. "How? Why?"

"Because we've had the same kind of lives. We come from the same place, Rick," Stephanie said with urgency.

"I don't see that at all," argued Rick.

"I know you don't. I don't expect you to. Because everything I've ever told you about me is a lie." Stephanie hung her head. She couldn't bear to look at him. At least this would be the last time she'd ever hurt him.

"Tell me, Steph," he said urgently. "I want to hear everything."

Stephanie hesitated, thinking over the enormity of what she was about to do. Everyone at Glenwood would know her story now. Rick put his hand under her chin and raised it, forcing her to look at him. His deep brown eyes were filled with concern.

"Rick, I'm not Alex's cousin. I'm her foster sister. This is the sixth foster home I've been in because my mother didn't want me. She gave me up when I was five."

Rick's face grew pale.

"What about your dad?" he asked holding on to her hands.

"I don't know who he was. I don't even know where my mother is now. Bruce has been trying to help me—he works for this agency that helps kids find their parents—but we haven't found out anything yet."

"But, Steph, please understand," Rick said tenderly. "I love you for you . . . right now. That's what's important. Not the past."

"But I'm a mess, Rick. A liar, a runaway. I've even been in jail." She wanted so badly to believe he still loved her, but he had to know everything.

"So was Isabelle, Steph, but I didn't love her less."

"Isabelle!" Stephanie's mind whirled in confusion. "Your sister?"

"My sister, heir to half the Forrester fortune."

"But she has everything. She's beautiful and smart and talented— "

"Steph, don't you see? So are you," Rick interrupted. "You just don't believe it, or don't want to believe it. Remember when I told you I was going to convince you some day what a terrific person you are?" He kissed her lightly on the lips, then pulled away. "I'm not about to give up on you. I believe in you, even if you don't."

Stephanie burst into tears and threw her arms around Rick. He held her close, stroking her hair.

"Oh, Rick, I love you so much. I have for ages, but I didn't believe you could love me, especially if you knew the truth."

"I love you more. You proved me right. I always thought you were one of the strongest people I'd ever met . . . not to mention beautiful and sexy, but we can go into that later."

"No, tell me now," laughed Stephanie, "Tell me now."

"Well, when you first came to Glenwood . . ."

Stephanie groaned. "Don't remind me. You thought I was Superjerk, right?"

"Not at all. In many ways you reminded me of Isabelle."

"Must have been my long blond hair and brilliant mind," quipped Stephanie.

Rick put his hand over her mouth. "Be quiet,

Stephanie. It's my turn." He started again. "Isabelle had a hard time growing up, too. It's not easy being a Forrester. My parents are wonderful people and supertalented. But they put a lot of pressure on Isabelle and me to be as great as they are. Now, maybe we will be someday, but we have to be able to live our lives and make our mistakes and learn what's best for us first. Mom and Dad always have everything all mapped out for us. That's hard to take."

Stephanie took his hand in hers and squeezed it gently. She could tell these admissions weren't easy for him

"When Isabelle was about sixteen," he continued emotionally, "she cracked from the pressure and completely rejected them. She ran away, got mixed up with a cult that was into some heavy drugs. My parents finally had the cult headquarters raided and closed down, but again Isabelle resented their interference and ran off. This time she toured the country as a rock band groupie."

Stephanie could feel her eyes bugging out of her head. This was the same beautiful Isabelle of the fairy-tale wedding! The one who was a rising star in the world of computer design! Whew!

"When did Isabelle start getting it together?" she asked in awe. "How did she do it?"

"Things started coming together for her the summer after she graduated from Glenwood. Most good people seem to survive their battles in the end."

"Isabelle didn't just survive, she triumphed," exclaimed Stephanie. "I guess that's why your parents are so proud of her."

"Yes . . . like they said, she's come a long way."

"Now it's your turn, huh?"

Rick snorted. "Yeah, I guess it is. Fortunately, I'm a little more stable than Isabelle so I've escaped a lot of what she went through, but my parents have already started in on me, and I'm feeling the pressure."

"How do you mean?" Stephanie asked.

Rick sighed and sat back in his chair. "Oh, they've already got me going to Harvard or Stanford, have mapped out graduate school for me after that, and are discussing where I might want to practice when I'm a big-deal corporate lawyer. Only trouble is they haven't bothered to ask me what I want to do." He ran his hands through his hair in despair. "I don't know what I want to do, though, and that drives them nuts, which in turn puts a lot of pressure on me to make decisions I don't feel ready to make. It's all crazy."

'I can't believe you have all these hassles," said Stephanie quietly, shaking her head in disbelief. "I thought you had the perfect storybook family."

Rick gave a short laugh. "In many ways, I have. We all love each other, and that's the most important thing, but no one's free of problems, Stephanie. It's how you work them out that counts."

"Don't tell me that," said Stephanie mournfully. "Seems like I just keep creating more and more problems for myself."

"No!" exclaimed Rick. Stephanie jumped, confused at his outburst. "No, Stephanie!" He grabbed her shoulders and shook her lightly.

"You haven't been listening to me," he continued almost harshly. "You must! It's important for you . . .

for us . . . that you understand this. If nothing else, give me a little credit. You keep painting this picture of yourself as a real loser and jerk. Why would I be interested in such a waste of time? Do I have so little going for me that I have to settle for one of society's charity cases?" He shook her again. "No, Steph. No, I don't. I want to be with you . . . I love you . . . for who you are. And that is definitely not a loser."

Stephanie looked up at him, her eyes filled with love and awe. Could it really be true? His face, though stern, was filled with caring. Genuine caring . . . for her.

"I've admired you from the first time I set eyes on you. Sure you were a tough and could be pretty obnoxious—make that very obnoxious—but that was just the surface. Below that I saw a fighter. A real fighter. You're always going to fight for what you believe in . . . " He took her face in his hands and stared deeply into her eyes. " . . . And you're going to win. I know that . . . and deep down inside . . . I think you know that, too."

Rick put his arms around her and pulled her in close to his chest. Stephanie could feel his heart pounding with the same crazy rhythm as hers. If Rick could believe in her, she could certainly start believing in herself. It seemed so easy with his love behind her. But wait a minute. She pulled back and stared at him for a second.

"What about Marcia?" she asked, feeling a flutter of insecurity course up through her. "You two seem to have a pretty cozy setup, or is it just my imagination that wherever you are, she is?"

Rick sighed. "Marcia . . . Marcia is just Marcia.

Everytime she's between boyfriends, like now, she latches on to me. I guess I'm sort of her security blanket or something."

Beautiful, perfect Marcia needs a security blanket, wondered Stephanie. Well, if Isabelle could have the kinds of problems she'd had, maybe Marcia had insecurities below the surface that she never let anyone see, either.

"But why did you take her to the Spring Fling?" queried Stephanie.

"I knew you were going to misinterpret that," Rick replied. "It was just another one of Marcia's games. When she found out I was going by myself, she went alone, too, and jumped me. It's hard to get rid of someone like her without making a scene."

"But what about the ring . . . I heard you gave her a ring, that you were going steady. Is that how you get rid of somebody?" Stephanie had pulled completely away and was staring at him. She'd given him her whole story. Now she wanted his.

Rick groaned. "That girl's wild, I tell you. I told my parents not to do it."

"Do what?"

"They're Marcia's godparents—our families go back a long way—and they decided to give her a birthstone ring for her birthday last week. Marcia's been doing a superheavy trip on me recently, so I figured she'd find some way to link that ring up with me. My parents thought I was nuts to even suggest she'd do such a thing. And I guess it does sound kind of crazy, but I know Marcia and, as you're learning, no trick is beyond her."

He smiled wearily at Stephanie. "May I get down

from the witness stand now, your honor? I promise I've told you everything there is to know."

Stephanie laughed. Her body felt light and buoyant, her mind free. "Just one more thing—how'd you know where to find me tonight? Were you behind us all that time?"

"Yes. Bruce told me you'd left with Kirk and that you seemed pretty upset. I figured I'd better check it out."

"That was some pretty fancy driving, Forrester," she said admiringly, punching him playfully in the chest.

"Hey, lady, you don't think my dad would let me own a car like that without at least a few driving lessons from the nation's best, do you?" He laughed. "I learned to drive high-powered cars from the same guy who taught Wes Thorsen. When I'd passed that test, then, and only then, would Dad hand over the keys."

"I should have known." Stephanie laughed. "The Forresters never do things by halves, huh?"

"Why should we?" asked Rick, helping her to her feet. The look in his eyes made Stephanie's heart pound uncontrollably.

"Let's go find somewhere a little more comfortable," he said, his voice deep in his throat. He led Stephanie into the living room and pulled her down on the couch beside him. For a moment they stared into each other's eyes. Stephanie felt as if they had both bared their souls. Now she had nothing to hide. And in spite of all she'd told him . . . Rick loved her. As if on cue, they wrapped their arms around each other. It felt so right, as if she'd finally come home.

No more barriers, no more guilt, no more lies.

"I love you, Rick," Stephanie murmured, burying her head in his neck. "I love you so much."

"Oh, Stephanie," he said, squeezing her so tightly she could hardly breathe. "I've wanted to hear you say that . . . so badly." His strong hands rubbed her back, moving in deep, slow circles. "Oh, I love you, too," he whispered.

Chapter Ten

Stephanie flexed her knees, shifted her weight forward onto her toes, and squinted across the net at her opponent. A trickle of sweat ran down her back. Then another. She'd been on the court for two and a half hours already, but there was just one more person to beat before the intermediate division of the tournament came to a close.

She watched Marcia toss the ball into the air and bring her racket down after it. A perfect serve. But Stephanie was ready. She swung evenly and firmly, hitting the ball dead center. It spun back over the net and landed just past the tip of Marcia's racket. She lunged for it, but missed.

"Advantage . . . Burroughs," shouted the referee. "And time out called by Miss Connors."

Stephanie groaned silently. This was match point. Why didn't Marcia just play it out . . . go for it? They were both exhausted, but stopping now could throw off her momentum.

Stephanie glanced up into the packed bleachers. When she saw Rick smiling down at her, her body filled with renewed energy. Her heart swelled. The whole gang sat behind him, plus Dr. and Mrs. Enomoto. They'd all given up a Saturday morning to come and cheer her on. They waved and whistled and stomped when they caught her eye.

"Quiet on the court, please. Quiet on the court."

Geez, this ref sounded as if he were practicing for Wimbledon or something. Stephanie wiped the sweat off her forehead and adjusted her headband as she walked over to the sidelines. She smiled and waved to her fans, the sun glinting off her bright red fingernails—all ten of them in perfect shape. A minute later, she was back in place on the court, her legs feeling like rubber. How much longer would they hold her up? How much longer could she keep her concentration? They'd gone to deuce on match point four times, and it looked as if they could go on like this forever. Stephanie could see the determination on Marcia's face.

Marcia bounced the ball slowly on the court, preparing to serve. All at once Stephanie felt eyes boring into her. She looked hastily around. Over half the high school was gathered in the bleachers or around the fence, but nothing seemed to be out of the ordinary. Then she caught a movement out of the corner of her eye. It was Kirk, standing alone at the edge of the bleachers. There eyes met, and he smiled—a wide, happy smile. Then he gave her the thumbs up.

Stephanie grinned back.

She turned to Marcia just as the ball sailed over the net right down the center line. Praying that her backhand wouldn't let her down, Stephanie went for it. She shot the ball back, but it was a sloppy return. Marcia ran forward and was on it in a second. The ball flew over the net. Again, Stephanie lunged and again she just got there in time. But she was on the defensive now, and that was bad—she mustn't let Marcia control the net. Panic fluttered in Stephanie's stomach, but she ignored it and steeled herself for the next shot.

The ball fell short, landing close to the net, and Stephanie made a snap decision. She was going to play up at the net like the boys did, just as Rick had shown her. Force Marcia back onto the defensive. She tore up to the net and lobbed the ball gently so it fell just on the other side. Stephanie could see the surprise on Marcia's face as she ran up for it. She managed to return it, but Stephanie could tell her opponent was thrown off balance. She was standing off to one corner, all Stephanie had to do was place that ball on the other side of the court—or at her feet.

Stephanie slammed the ball hard, and Marcia had to leap back to keep it from hitting her feet. Her racket scooped the court, sending the ball back across the net in a wobbly return. Now Marcia was even farther over the right of the court.

Slowly and deliberately, Stephanie brought her racket back into position. When the ball was at waist level, she swung, making contact with a solid *thwack*. The ball took off like a rocket and spun over the net with only inches to spare, landing deep in the far left corner. There was no way Marcia could get it. She didn't even try.

"Game to Miss Burroughs," announced the ref. "Congratulations, Miss Burroughs. You're the new intermediate intramural tennis champion of Glenwood High School. Please come forward and accept your award."

Stephanie couldn't believe it. She'd won! She'd won!

Stephanie shook Marcia's limp hand, then took the envelope handed to her by the principal. A hundred-dollar gift certificate to the Emporium!

"We're all very proud of you, Stephanie," he said, smiling broadly. "You're an asset to Glenwood High. Congratulations." Then he placed the intramural tennis trophy in her hands. Stephanie stared at it reverently. Her own trophy. Her very own trophy. She ran the shiny metal down her sleeve for a quick polish. She really was good at something.

Stephanie grinned. "Thanks a lot, Mr. Morrison." Then she turned to the roaring crowd and waved. Suddenly she was surrounded by friends and classmates pounding her on the back and hugging her. She caught Alex's eye over the heads, and the two girls stared at each other for a long second. Tears stood in both their eyes.

"Way to go, Steph," said Rick, scooping her up in his arms and swinging her around. "You were terrific."

Stephanie wrapped her arms around him and buried her head in his neck. She never knew she could be so happy.

"Okay, everyone, back to our house for a victory

barbecue," announced Mrs. Enomoto.

Again they all cheered and dashed for their cars, and Stephanie was swept along with the crowd.

For the next two hours the Frisbee didn't stop as Justin, Rick, Craig, and Carl challenged each other to more and more difficult shots in the Enomotos' backyard. Eventually Alex played the winner and won, while Stephanie cheered her on madly from the sidelines. Lori set up croquet, and for the next hour they devoured the juicy hot dogs and hamburgers that came sizzling off Dr. Enomoto's grill while taking turns playing rounds of croquet, which Elaine finally won.

"So, what are you going to get with your gift certificate, Steph?" asked Kit, flopping down on the grass under the big cottonwood tree. The others soon joined her, everyone exhausted but beaming with happiness. Stephanie was sorry Wes wasn't there for Alex's sake, but as usual, he was racing.

"Well," began Stephanie shyly. "Let's just say I could sure use some good advice."

"Weren't we planning another expedition to the Emporium next week, gang?" Alex said, giving everyone a big wink.

"You bet," Elaine chimed in. "We're not about to let her spend that wad of dough without us."

"Plus it's the last week of sales," added Lori. "So you'll get some great deals."

"Am I invited?" asked Rick, his brown eyes filled with mock pleading.

"Not a chance," replied Kit. "Some territory is still private to us girls, right?" All the boys groaned.

"Right," Alex agreed. "But don't worry, you'll get to enjoy the results."

"And I get the feeling you'll probably see her more than we will, anyway," said Elaine.

"I plan to," said Rick, slipping his arm around Stephanie and holding her close. She blushed and laughed, and everyone cracked up.

"Hey, what are you going to do with your trophy, Steph?" Justin asked.

"I think you should melt it down and make matching rings for all your very best friends," quipped Kit.

Again Stephanie giggled, then sobered. "No, I'll show you what I'm going to do with it."

She picked up her trophy and started upstairs. They all followed, crowding into her room after her. Stephanie walked over to the window sill and placed it beside Noodle's chess trophy.

Everyone clapped, and Mrs. Enomoto smiled warmly at Stephanie through her tears.

"Well, I guess I ought to put a shelf up in here," said Dr. Enomoto, surveying the empty walls. "Looks like you could use it."

Stephanie's cheeks reddened. "Thanks . . . Dad."

Dr. Enomoto put his arms around Stephanie's shoulders and hugged her affectionately.

"Mr. Emerson suggested I compete in the annual Glenwood Tennis Tournament this summer," added Stephanie shyly.

"So you'll definitely need that shelf for all your trophies," said Alex, clapping Stephanie on the back.

"Don't you think it's the perfect time to give her our presents?" asked Rick, turning to Alex. Alex disappeared and was back in a second with two long tubes.

Stephanie opened the one from Alex first and unrolled a huge poster of Martina Navratilova holding up her Wimbledon trophy.

"Wow, Alex, thanks!" exclaimed Stephanie.

"I gave you Navratilova because she's the best . . . and I think you're the best," Alex proclaimed.

"Thanks, Sis," Stephanie said, smiling at the bare walls. "This old room sure could use a poster or two, huh?"

"Good," said Rick, handing her the second roll. " 'Cause here's my present." Stephanie opened it to find another poster, this one of Chris Evert Lloyd executing her famous two-handed backhand.

"Are you trying to tell me this is what my backhand should really look like?" joked Stephanie. Everyone laughed.

"If your backhand ever looks like that," shot back Rick, "I'm not getting anywhere near you on the court. No way!" He hesitated, then smiled warmly at Stephanie. "I gave you Chrissy," he continued, "because she's so tough . . . and so beautiful." He grinned mischievously at her.

Stephanie's cheeks went bright red, and she practically choked with pleasure. Suddenly, Gazpacho came scampering into the room.

"Hey, look who's rushed in to congratulate you, too," Rick said, laughing. He picked up the kitten, handing him to Stephanie. Cradling Gazpacho in one arm, her other arm around Rick, Stephanie looked out at her friends, her family, her home. She felt like Cinderella, transformed after she'd found her prince. She was filled with joy. Now all she had to do was find her mother. Once she found her mom, she could bring the past up to the present. Then she could face the future without questions, without hesitation. To find her mother...

Stephanie turned her thoughts back to Rick and squeezed him with all her strength. With Rick's love behind her there was no way she could fail. Of that she was certain. Stephanie relaxed completely against him, feeling a warm, beautiful sun rising over the battleground of her soul.

SENIORS